The American Years

The American Years
Dunoon & the US Navy

Andrene Messersmith

Argyll
publishing

© 2003 Andrene Messersmith

Argyll Publishing
Glendaruel
Argyll PA22 3AE
Scotland
www.skoobe.biz

British Library Cataloguing-in-Publication Data.

A catalogue record for this book is available from the British Library.

ISBN 1 902831 61 6

Origination Cordfall Ltd, Glasgow

Printing Bell & Bain Ltd, Glasgow

Acknowledgements

My heartfelt thanks to all of the contributors for their enthusiastic participation. Without their input, this book would not be the historical record that it is.

My gratitude for help and kind permission goes to Marion Inglis at the *Dunoon Observer* and to George Giarchi for use of research material in his book *Between McAlpine and Polaris*.

Thanks are also due to John Stirling at Cowal Heritage Trust Museum for unlimited help.

Thanks to Derek and Jennifer for their faith, to my mother for her encouragement and to my husband Ralph for his loving support.

Andrene Messersmith
July 2003

Even in the middle of winter, when the hills may be covered in snow and Dunoon, set out beneath them, is etched by the long rays of the winter sun so that it takes on the sharp clarity of a Japanese engraving, Dunoon is a pleasant place to be in.

'In the green and leafy month of May, when the first, fresh colours of early summer are as yet untarnished by the heat of the dog days; or in October when a warm, pale-golden glow illuminates the rich reds and browns of our Scottish autumn.'

Maurice Lindsay
The Dunoon Guide 1960

Contents

Stepping off the gangway of USS *Holland* in the Holy Loch

FOREWORD
The Monster in the Loch

George Robertson

(The Rt Hon Lord Robertson of Port Ellen,
Secretary General, NATO)

I watched the arrival of the first Polaris submarine in the Holy Loch in 1961 when I was 15 and by a complete fluke of timing I followed, on a Western Ferry, the last departing submarine out of the Loch in 1991. It was a complete coincidence, being the day after Dunoon Grammar School's 350th Anniversary Dinner. But it was fitting because these submarines in that quiet Highland loch were to change the course of my life completely and permanently.

I had been interested in politics before then. The school had that tradition through its debating society. And the spirit of John Smith lingered on after he went to university. But the arrival of the Americans, and in particular the legions who descended on the town to protest, brought big-time politics to Dunoon and my young life in a huge way.

The American families took the school by storm. Children with accents you could cut with a knife, and names so exotic as to be unpronounceable took to local life like ducks to water. Most were used to an itinerant life and had few inhibitions. They could speak the language (sort of) and were instantly at home.

Dunoon Grammar School was involved in 1963 in a school ship project with over 800 students embarking on the former liner and troop-ship *Devonia*. The idea was an educational cruise to the Baltic region. The subsidised cost was so reasonable that half the DGS contingent was American – despite the irony that one port of call was to be Leningrad, a presumed target for the parental missiles.

Because of my age I was made a ship's prefect, an early heavy responsibility since most of the teachers repaired to the duty-free bars as soon as we left territorial waters. It was a nightmare, with American, Scottish and Irish delinquents causing diplomatic havoc in Oslo, Copenhagen, Helsinki, and in very Soviet Leningrad.

Russia was prepared for a military invasion of millions of troops and they could shadow and track every move of individual tourists. What they could not cope with was 800 school children who came to get Russian souvenirs and who found that the easiest way to get them was to trade the clothes they were wearing. I have always wondered what one Soviet citizen did with the American bomber-jacket he got in exchange for a painted box. After all it was emblazoned with a huge Polaris missile and the legend 'USS *Hunley* – we serve to preserve peace'.

The culmination was the departure from the dock. Russian school children were bussed in to fraternally wave goodbye and were prevented from joining us by a line of Russian policemen. Our crowd were issued with rolls of streamers, but it was soon found that if they were licked they did not open and were natty projectiles. Every hit on a policeman raised a genuine cheer from our Russian compatriots.

About thirty years later I returned to Leningrad, on the eve of its renaming as St Petersburg, this time as a VIP. I took the big gamble of telling the tale of the dock. To my surprise an elderly volunteer interpreter told she me had been one of the teachers and the younger official who organised our visit said she remembered being transported to see the ships off.

But my whole-life change was to come from the demonstrators who came to stop the submarines coming and staying. They came in their thousands to a town and an obscure loch they had never heard of. Great national figures ended up in Dunoon – MPs, trade union leaders, household names from the TV and press. They even had hand-made songs. 'You canny spend a dollar when you're deid' and 'There's a high road to Gourock and a ferry to Dunoon, and the whole world will be watching when we're marching through the toon' . It was a travelling political fairground and I was captivated.

It was not easy, or risk free. I thought it was excitement of the most exquisite sort. My father, also George Robertson and who died last year, was the local head of CID and second in command of Dunoon police. He was less than enchanted by his son and namesake's political adventure. While I was using my bicycle to find campsites for my new 'friends', he was

planning to thwart the civil disobedience. While I was on the marches, he was arresting those who sat and blocked the road at Ardnadam Pier. I was not popular at home.

As I grew up I grew unconvinced by the slogans. 'Ban The Bomb' looked neat on a banner, but was hardly a basis for a real-world policy. I parted company with the emotional and improbable 'if we do it, the world will follow' school. However I have never, to this day, lost my early passion to make the world safer and all weapons less needed. It still motivates my life today.

It was during this period that I teamed up with a youthful, crew-cutted Boys-Brigader called Brian Wilson. He too caught the heady excitement of top-level protest politics and we both joined the 'ban the bomb' Scottish National Party. I fell out with and from them after a year but Brian lingered a little longer till we were both at Dundee University. Then we both joined force again against them. And now we are together again – as members of Her Majesty's Privy Council!

Apart from the impact on my father's police career, caused by some small minded superiors, I regret none of these long-ago anti-Polaris days. I grew up politically very fast. I got politics into the bloodstream. I became absorbed in knowing about one of the great issues of our age, which has since dominated my career and interests.

In addition, I was to gain immense self-confidence from being about people with strong views. That's a great start to life, and I never pretend it did not exist. In fact in the new democracies I now visit across the world I tell some pretty astounded audiences of my political start in life and the merit of getting involved and learning and changing as I did.

Last year President George W Bush held a dinner in

my honour in the White House. Defence Secretary Don Rumsfeld asked across the table if I came from near the nuclear base in Scotland. I said yes, and that I had actually come into politics by protesting against US submarines. A pretty amazed President said, 'Did you know that, Don?' Don said no. I swiftly pointed to the political early days of Portuguese Prime Minister Barosso (Maoist), Spanish Foreign Minister Pique (Spanish Communist Party) and I didn't have time to get to German Foreign Minister Fischer, Robin Cook or Gordon Brown, when the President, born the same year as me, interrupted. 'As everyone knows, I was raising hell at that age, so let's ignore these early days.'

So today I lead NATO, the most successful defence alliance in world history. I am Chairman of the NATO/Russia Council with 19 NATO nations and Russia sitting as equals round my table, and from 1997 to 1999 I was responsible for all of Britain's defences, including its four nuclear ballistic missile submarines. But it all started in Dunoon when the Americans arrived forty years ago. Strange how life turns out.

I know this book will reawaken new interest and old memories of an event which was to change the character of Dunoon, its Grammar School and many, many individual lives. The arrival of the Americans in the Holy Loch was a huge happening in Scottish and even international terms, but in its human impact it was most marked on those in the Cowal locality. I offer my own personal memoir – and how it all affected my life and career – but in the following pages others tell their colourful tales. This is a significant part of Scotland's rich social history – and a great read as well.

A bomber jacket bearing these badges – sought after in Soviet Russia!

Permission: Jim Collins

Holy Loch 1966 and the arrival of USS *Simon Lake* to take over from USS *Hunley*. The gentleman wearing the kilt is Provost of Dunoon Gordon Trapp. He gives his account of an unusual day on page 41

Introduction

In March 1961, a crowd of people gathered along the shoreline in the little Argyllshire town of Dunoon to watch the future arrive, in the form of the USS *Proteus*. They were unsure what this would look like but expected it to be rather glossy and shiny, somehow – perhaps a large white liner steaming along carrying hordes of waving sailors. Instead they saw a grey military shape appear on the horizon and chug towards the nearby Holy Loch, looking really rather insignificant and disappointing.

Nonetheless this symbol did carry the future for many people whose lives and destinies would change when it reached its destination and sent out its tendrils into the surrounding area, tendrils that grew into branches that intertwined with the local undergrowth in an irrevocable way.

When a secret decision was made by the British government in 1960, under pressure from the Eisenhower government, to allow an American Polaris base in Scotland, it was a political one. If we were to live in alliance with America, she had to have her way about where she set up camp. It was a trade-off and it was believed that to refuse, left us alone and vulnerable in the fast developing nuclear world. Not everyone accepted this theory and many argued that it propelled us into the front line, and amounted to a provocation to the Soviet empire. But the fact remained that our local population was about to increase greatly with Americans, people with whom we shared culture and language.

However in the early sixties the differences between us, in our ways of life and traditions, were a greater divide. Personal travel and communication were not nearly as advanced as today, and many of us had never met an American. We had plenty of preconceptions though, and prejudices. And the servicemen had theirs.

This book is really about how in the early days we tried to adjust to each other and befriend, whatever our political views. It is the human experiences behind the political decisions that are explained here in people's own words. This is not an academic or social analysis of the effects of the Base, which have been carried out so expertly in other publications such as GG Giarchi's *Between McAlpine and Polaris*. It is neither a defence of nor an attack on the politics of the matter. It is a book of personal outlines to give the reader some insight into what it was like to live in those times, from both sides, and for those of us who experienced it ourselves, to reflect.

WEST BAY, DUNOON.

To ONE I LOVE from DUNOON

DUNOON FROM WEST BAY

Scenes of Dunoon as a 'doon the watter' resort in the 1950s

Dunoon, as the guidebook of 1960 said, 'caters for the wishes and tastes of almost every imaginable kind of holidaymaker'

American Dream World

When I was a child, in the fifties, my father would occasionally bring home a bundle of large, glossy American magazines. I would turn the shiny pages of these treasures. Sculptured women and chiselled men stared out of the adverts, her mink coat draped around her elegant shoulders, his coat hung casually over the shoulder of his expensive tuxedo, behind them an endless, gleaming Cadillac, complete with tail fins. A pleasant chemical scent came off the full colour printing, a rich, luxuriant smell of opulence and sophistication. For me, these pages were America.

It was a dream world that most young people aspired to in bland postwar Britain, a country whose older population was eager to stabilise in family life and modest ambitions. It was a world obsessed with a consumerism depicted as the 'pursuit of happiness'.

The cinema was, of course, a fount of our dreams. Hollywood films of the decade reflected a postwar American prosperity and growth. It was a land of plenty that we perceived, where the population enjoyed an increasingly high standard of living, where the kids went to drive-in movies, ate hamburgers and hot dogs, and went to wonderful summer camps. Even the depiction of poverty there seemed glamorous. We watched American comedy on our black and white TVs and loved it. The Phil Silvers show, Jack Benny, Shelly Berman, Burns and Allen were all larger than life figures and somehow special in a starry way. We

children were avid fans of the 'Lone Ranger', 'Champion the Wonder Horse' and Roy Rogers and Trigger.

Plenty of Scots had emigrated to a new life in America, but it was a far more monumental decision in those days before cheap jet travel. 'Abroad' was a far more distant concept in the fifties. We had heard of New York and Hollywood, Texas, California, the Great Plains, the Badlands – and what romantic visions these names produced in our minds! When we heard that Americans were coming to live with us, we, children especially, imbued these ordinary Americans with all the mystical otherness of people from another planet.

Was this true also for the American families who were told of their new posting in Scotland? What sort of place were they coming to?

The Holy Loch itself is an exquisitely beautiful stretch of water surrounded by heather-clad hills. Its name came from the time of the Crusades when a ship sank there emptying its cargo of earth from the Holy Land into the deep water. The population around its edges enjoyed a scenic panorama in their daily lives. Their children played safely and attended village schools. The Loch was filled with yachts and pleasure steamers in the summer. The local buses gave a good service into Dunoon and small local shops provided well. The residents of Sandbank enjoyed the typical life of a small Scottish village. You can travel along the coast to Dunoon from there or over the High Road, both routes traversing lovely landscapes.

Dunoon nestles on the Cowal peninsula. It is cosily tucked into the nooks and crannies and glens of the surrounding hills and beaded along the coastline, reaching south to the villages of Innellan and Toward and north to Sandbank. It has a solid Victorian centre with well-designed streets and attractive houses. It has a rich history in its development, mainly growing into its present outlines when rich Glasgow merchants chose to build their solid villas in its most desirable spots in the 1800s and then the businesses to service them appeared. When holidays became possible for working class people boarding houses and hotels were built to meet these needs and families bought little 'but 'n bens' to house enormous families for the Glasgow fair fortnight. What a treat to leave the filthy cities, travel on a ferry stacked with passengers in holiday mood, dancing to the music of little bands of musicians and breathing the first bracing gulps of seaside air.

As a seaside town in the 1950s Dunoon life brightened considerably in the summer months. The surrounding area of Cowal was full of beauty and magical places. As children we knew the town like the back of our hands and could live a life of secure and familiar routine in a safe environment. Summer was an outdoor life. We spent a lot of it on the shingled beach, swimming in the bracing waters of the Clyde. There were multiple little huts dotted along the shoreline where we hired deck chairs, rowing boats and little puttering motor launches. The river was teaming with

ferries and paddle steamers and holidaymakers packed the beach and the promenade. There was a beautiful 1930s Art Deco bathing lido in the West Bay, its roof a tarmaced sunspot, but its lower steps in shadow most of the day. The older bathers would swim out to its large raft and sunbathe. We could visit its cafe for orange squash afterwards. Opposite lay the beautiful Morag's Fairy Glen, romantic and secluded, for a cool stroll through greenery. The swing park was nearby, beside the paddling pool, a muddy-watered venue for toddlers to develop their immune systems in a way that would be unthinkable now! On the rainy days the La Scala picture house was the ideal place to spend the afternoon. There was always a double programme and it was changed three times a week, so if you had enough pocket money you could pass a rainy week in escapism.

In the Dunoon guide for 1960, page after page of adverts large and small for hotels, boarding houses and bed and breakfast illustrate the town's reliance on holidaymakers especially at the Glasgow Fair and Cowal Games weekend. 45,000 passengers a year were crossing the Clyde on car ferries. Maurice Lindsay, author of the *Guide to Dunoon* writes,

But the wise tourist will not wish simply to pass through Dunoon. Not only is it an excellent touring centre – indeed, by far the best on the Clyde – but it caters for the wishes and tastes of almost every imaginable kind of holidaymaker; and the holidaymaker who comes to stay will want to know something of the past which has brought into being this friendly, welcoming little town that today exists mainly for his pleasure.

The influx of visitors brought a vibrancy and stimulus to the community. Things 'livened up' in the summer. GG Giarchi writes of the town swelling to three times its population.

The car wasn't considered a necessity then in Dunoon as people could walk everywhere. It was a luxury for Sunday runs to Toward or Ardentinny. Many mothers walked to the shops and home, with the 'messages'. Anything heavy was delivered by the obliging family businesses in the town. There was no supermarket. Shop assistants served you. Milk was delivered to everyone by the local farms. A high proportion of us attended church.

We went home on winter nights to coal fires, paraffin heaters and electric fires dotted around the house, to keep us warm. It did not make for an even, comfortable heat around the home. In fact passing from kitchen coal fire to bathroom paraffin fire meant a shivery trip through the freezing hall. Taking a bath (no-one had a shower) meant leaving a fug-filled bathroom, to traverse the freezing stairs, and hover over the electric bars till one's hair dried. In bed, if you were lucky, you had one hot spot around the hot water bottle your mum had thoughtfully placed amidst acres of freezing sheets. It wasn't unusual that people had a bath and washed their hair once a week only.

You awoke in the morning under the required heavy pile of blankets, (no-one knew what a duvet was) and surveyed the beautiful frosted leaf patterns on the inside of the window, your breath visible in the air.

Young peoples' social lives at that time revolved around Church socials and dancing to the 'Meltones' or the 'Clyde Valley Stompers' at the small pavilion hall. Parents were very involved in organising and chaperoning these events. Any drinking in the younger generation was a more furtive activity in those different days. Fifties Britain still reigned in 1961. Any escapades were likely to come to the attention of parents and teachers, and only the boldest and bravest showed any rebellious attitude. The consequences could be too daunting!

Older children were beginning to connect with the wider world through music, their very own music, for the first time, with their own record players and transistor radios. When my father presented my sister and I with an old wireless set for our room in 1961, we rapidly tuned its old-fashioned dial to Radio Luxembourg. When we heard the sound of 'Poetry in Motion' coming over the airwaves we thought we'd been given a passport to teenage heaven. We could listen to all the pop music we wanted, late into the night. Sometimes we found the American Forces network in Europe, fiddling with that dial. The novelty of television brought even more structure to the week as our lives made room for our favourite programmes there as well as Radio. Scotland's own popular culture in TV's 'Dr Finlay's Casebook'. Singers like Kenneth McKellar and Andy Stewart were part of the national scene.

So what impact did the news, that an American Polaris Missile Base was coming to stay, have on the population of a small Scottish town, of around ten thousand souls as the sixties decade began? It had capacity for destruction that was beyond our imagination and it was coming to a place near us.

The local newspaper, normally concerned with matters parochial, rose to the occasion under the editorship of the late William Inglis. In the week after the government announcement (November 12th, 1960) the editorial in the *Dunoon Observer and Argyllshire Standard* stated:

> One of the most serious utterances ever made by any British Prime Minister since Sir Winston told of the retreat from Dunkirk, was that issued by Mr Macmillan a week ago when he announced his Government's agreement to permit an American Polaris Base in this country – in the Holy Loch, to be exact.

> That the announcement has murdered sleep among many thinking men and women in Britain is plain by the large amount of space in the daily press and the number of individuals who have written letters on the subject. The writers have been men and women of different walks of life and every shade of public opinion. There is no doubt whatever that grave fears exist all over Britain on the siting of a base in these Islands, and the Prime Minister's assurances in recent days in the House have not allayed these fears one whit.

It has been argued that polarised submarines will be a stabilising factor in the arms race. But the truth is there can be none. When the cities of Hiroshima and Nagasaki were wiped out by the first atomic bombs that was to be the end of such warfare. The passing years have not proved it so. Sooner or later some traitor betrays for wealth the invention, and the enemy soon possesses an ever bigger and better bomb. Is there anything to stop this happening again?

These words evoke the chilling effect the news had. Everyone had fears about the huge changes that would be imposed by this base. It was a time close enough to the war for the memories of visiting military to colour the expectations. On one hand it may bring riches to the town's economy. On the other hand these were different times. Would our peace be shattered? Would the children be safe? Would all the immorality that has surrounded military bases throughout history be brought to our doors? There was no housing especially for them so were they going to overwhelm us? But uppermost in all our minds was the fact that this was a Polaris weapons base. It had capacity for destruction that was beyond our imagination. It was coming to a place near us.

It is hard to imagine now how much the Cold War dominated our national news then and occupied the pundits. The balance of power tipped back and forth between America and Russia each week, and the tensions were palpable in the background of daily life. Behind the Iron Curtain was the enemy of our way of life and freedom, we were told, and we had to match his powers to prevent his domination of the world. The 'Space Race' was underway. The nuclear age had begun; our eyes were on the hands of the clock. As children we were aware of it but not with intensity until the news of the base broke. This was something that was a distant rumble before 1961, but after, it became rather more personal.

It all happened suddenly. In the months before, an American ship had anchored off Dunoon and there had been a dollar spending spree. People now looked back at that cynically, as a 'softener' to manipulate the town's reactions. Dunoon was suddenly the focus of international attention and it wasn't all pleasant. Reporters asked our opinions, but underlying all this was the feeling that we were the dupes that would be sitting on a bomb, a nuclear one at that. There could be an accident. Would our waters be polluted and poisoned? What secret things would be done to us?! Would we be exposed to high levels of radiation? No-one seemed to give a straight answer to the question of safety.

Dunoon Town Council had debated the dangers but far from vigorously protesting seemed to take the line of least resistance. It could be said that as a Town Council its concerns must lie with the prospects for business in such monumental matters. It was the Argyll County Council that, though divided, had agreed to oppose the siting of the base in Holy Loch. Indeed a County Councillor Robertson had resigned from the local Hospital Board because it had not discussed the Polaris base. He stated to the local newspaper,

One of our hospitals is situated within 500 yards of the moorings for the Polaris missiles. In view of the misleading statements and inaccurate reports at the recent meeting of Dunoon Town Council, I am alarmed that our Hospitals Board, hospitals staffs, and local doctors have received no instructions whatsoever regarding the treatment, especially of children, in the event of the very real probability of a serious radioactive fallout. Hospital beds in the area are not even adequate for present needs. The most serious mis-statement made at the Town Council meeting was that a radioactive cloud would not travel beyond the shores of the Loch. With a suitable wind the cloud could travel a distance of 25 miles doing damage to the thyroid glands of children and causing serious consequences to any person within a 10 mile radius.

Moreover, people had approached this Councillor about who would pay compensation for any accidents involving radiation leaks, as their insurance companies refused to take on this risk. The advice was that the American Government would be liable as operators of the Base, under the Licensing and Insurance Act that had come into force in April 1960. But this was not reassuring.

A letter writer in The Safety Valve (the letters column of the *Dunoon Observer*) in March, 1961, opined,

Everyone else, including the people of America

on TV, appears to have heard the plans for evacuation of this district in the event of a nuclear mishap with the exception of ourselves who live nearest. I think it is time that a public meeting was called to give us the true facts, attended by our MP and County and Burgh officials.

Meanwhile the British Minister of Defence stated that this would not be a base but 'a few buoys in a sea loch to which a depot ship will moor'. This obfuscation only served to incense. Extracts from a letter to the Safety Valve expressed this well on 21st December 1961:

> May I remind readers that each of these missiles contains the explosive power equal to 1,000,000 tons of TNT – a happy thought indeed. Again we have been reassured that an accidental explosion is almost impossible. You will note that this is a qualified statement, mainly because their understanding of the power that they have unleashed is not complete. The statement by the Town Clerk was a revealing document. It was also a very naïve one. The piece de resistance was in the paragraph dealing with the effects of radiation. This we are assured is not lethal, but would merely have a genetic effect; in other words, we can tolerate a future race of abnormal children in return for the benefits conferred.

'Experts' tried to calm local fears but rumours abounded about us all being blown to Kingdom Come in our beds. The British government had imposed this fate on the town. We were, it was said, target number one on Russia's list, if things tipped over into conflict. Their weapons arsenal was aimed at Holy Loch and we'd be 'collateral damage' by intention or mistake and we felt helpless against it.

A Hunter's Quay resident wrote,

> It would appear that quite a number who applaud the decision have nostalgic memories of the booming war years and are prepared to stifle all moral scruples and with true ostrich escapism really believe that tragedy cannot overtake us. There are others who hold that the provision of an anchorage in the Holy Loch is necessary in order to bargain with with the USSR. This is quite fallacious. In fact the position is reversed. Russia has made it quite clear that she regards this Polaris Base as a provocative act, and that she has made her intention towards Britain and this area in particular quite clear.
> I do not believe that the public are sufficiently aware of the fact that this Polaris anchorage is not a NATO project but is a base being held on our territory by a Foreign Power, over which we have obviously the minimum control.

An Innellan resident obviously felt in the minority in the same Safety Valve column.

May I join in the Polaris controversy just to

An American sailor returning to USS *Proteus* steps over closely packed anti-Polaris demonstrators at Ardnadam Pier, May 1961

give my point of view, as this is still a free country.

For all practical purposes we are in partnership with America and others and to be a partner one must need to share the expense and the risk in some way. The Polaris submarine is at once one of the best defensive weapons available, simply because it has a roving commission and even the Russians do not know where this submarine is at any given time, whereas fixed strong points can be liquidated at very short notice.

It is all very well for some people to say Don't bring the base here, Send it north or south, Let the other fellow take the risk. But Great Britain is a very small island and should war come, most of us, North and South could say goodbye. Our surest safeguard is to be in a position of strength, and so be able to negotiate with Russia from strength, not weakness. Here's hoping we shall be successful.

The military needs of the State overruled our civil rights as residents of the area. No amount of protest was going to change it, it seemed.

Protest in those days was a more radical concept and not readily evident in Dunoon. The Campaign for Nuclear Disarmament (CND) made strenuous efforts and set up many strong demonstrations. This tended to feel like a double invasion to Dunoon people. These marchers were often dismissed as Beatniks, but when one studies the photos one can see a cross-section of ages and dress of the time. There were older conventionally dressed men and women, deeply concerned for their grandchildren's future. Predominantly students and teenagers made up the crowds and some of them were from Dunoon. There were a number of prominent politicians and Scots clergy leading the marches such as the Reverend James Curry and the Reverend George Macleod. Many trade unions were represented. A series of sit-downs lead to many arrests which were processed in the Sheriff Court alongside the first Americans who got into brawls in their first days ashore.

The issue of 'the Bomb' had radicalised many young people and given birth to the CND movement. This outpost of a foreign power disturbed them. Some marched against it and attended peace vigils. Furthermore the political map of Scotland with its strong working class Clydeside Socialism and left-wing politics did not provide a comfortable neighbourhood for a colony of post-McCarthy America. Socialism was one step from Communism in American culture. No American could travel to Russia without arousing his State's suspicion. The Iron Curtain worked both ways. When the second ship, the USS *Hunley* arrived in 1963, a *Daily Worker* journalist, a Mr Stein was refused permission to attend a press conference held by Captain Syverson and left on Ardnadam pier, so threatening a presence was he considered. The American press tended to report on the CND protesters as a subversive force.

When local meetings were held about the Base, it was often highly resented by locals when a contingent of anti-Polaris supporters turned up, as recorded in the following letter from a Blairmore resident to the Safety Valve columns on 17th December 1960.

Sir,

The report in your paper of 17t inst. on the Polaris meeting at Strone is most misleading. The correct version is that the meeting was attended by a few local residents, greatly outnumbered by an influx of strangers brought in from other districts. This meeting in no way represented the opinion of Kilmun, Strone or Blairmore but otherwise, true to the pattern followed by the organisers, the Scottish Council of Nuclear Disarmament, so called by the self-appointed founders some three years ago.

The main point of this letter is to express the hope that when our American friends do arrive we will not witness the spectacle of these objectors vieing with each other for favours. It is known that the American people work hard and play hard; social life forms an important part of their life. They not only think that their children are worth living for, they think their children worth fighting for. Our Education Authority will no doubt, give consideration to the placing of their children only in those schools where it is known they will not be indoctrinated with Socialist defeatism.

The *Proteus* set down anchor. A few days later the first submarine, the *USS Patrick Henry* arrived alongside for a change of crew, each Polaris sub having two crews assigned to it, the Blue crew and the Gold Crew. It took some bravery to sit down and refuse to move or take to a canoe and paddle towards the *Proteus*. Captain Arthur Bivens, then a young officer sent to Holy Loch in March 1961, for the first crew change, recalls,

Hundreds of anti-nuclear demonstrators were on hand along with the press to complicate the crew relief. Some of them paddled out in kayaks to harass or even board the ship. We had to develop new procedures to handle this kind of activity. Our Repel Boarders Bill was too violent and deadly for demonstrators. We warned them not to touch the ship and if they climbed aboard we were instructed to take them into custody and then hand them over to the British Constabulary. We also greased the top of our upper rudder to foil their attempts to climb up and perch on it. The majority sat down outside the gate to the pier at Ardnadam and tried to block access. The British constables were quite efficient and the demonstrators were mostly peaceful, shouting 'No Polaris' as we picked our way through them.

The protests gained in momentum but there was a feeling of fatalism. The older generation knew that governments follow their agendas despite public opinion. There were many older local people that were disturbed by the idea of a military front being once again set up close to home and war tensions, so

Demonstrators against the base took to the waters of Holy Loch in canoes and achieved national press coverage for their brave if foolhardy tactics. Their actions ended with the inevitable outcome – being arrested

A young activist in the shape of local man
Brian Wilson addresses CND demonstrators
at Ardnadam in 1977. Brian later went on to
become a Member of Parliament and
government minister

Brian Wilson MP

I vividly remember the arrival of the *Proteus*
and the debates, locally as well as nationally,
which that event gave rise to. The demonstrations which greeted the creation of the
Polaris base brought a huge range of people
and ideas, which otherwise we would not have
had direct contact with, to Dunoon. All of
that helped to shape my subsequent outlook,
interests and friendships.

The presence of Americans in Dunoon
Grammar School was a very positive part of
my formative years. While I never liked the
reason for them being there, they brought a
whole range of different values and interests
to which we would not normally have been
exposed. They made Dunoon a more
interesting place to grow up in and gave me an
early awareness that American people are
often a lot better than American foreign
policy!

© Herald & Evening Times (Newsquest) Ltd

Two US navy personnel pass the demonstrators

The American Years

Headscarves and bunnets among the demonstrators belie the 'beatnik' tag ascribed by some locals

do you want to be annihilated?

© Herald & Evening Times (Newsquest) Ltd

Padye Girard (née Porchetta) was a teenager when the TV reporters arrived to record local reaction to the news of the base

One day, while trotting along Argyll Street, I bumped into a TV crew, or really one man and a camera man. As most of us had only had a television set a few years this was a most unexpected and probably first time occurrence of live TV broadcasting from Dunoon.

I think it would be on Wednesday afternoon, the town's half day, because the street was as usual – you could shoot a cannonball down it, and not hit a soul. I can distinctly remember what I was wearing – a red suedette jacket with cream jeans, my hair a mass of natural curls, and as usual had my collie dog, Spot, in tow.

The interviewer, who I think may have been Raymond Baxter, but was certainly a big raw-boned man, posed me kneeling on one knee, hand resting on faithful collie's head and posed the question, 'What do you think of an American fleet of 1000 men coming to the Holy Loch?' There was little coverage of global happenings and transatlantic events in these days. My vision of Americans would be of movie stars, probably James Dean, so I blithely said, 'I reckon the local boys will have to pull up their socks!'

The term 'sound bite' had not been invented in those days, but of course that's exactly what it was. That night the BBC broadcast the transmission – serious debate, then me.

The next day I got a whiff of how the women who collaborated with the Nazis must have felt. I worked in the family hairdressing salon where all the young bloods came to get their haircut. It was like the run at Pamplona! The men of Dunoon came in like raging bulls, to confront me for my disloyalty. Many stood before me and pantomimed pulling up their socks and the guys that had least to offer, were the most vociferous in their annoyance! Even older men, who had obviously suffered from the 'over-paid, over-sexed and over here' effects from the last war, took me to task. It was quite daunting for the shy reserved girl I was then, and I supposed I wouldn't get asked to dance in the aircraft hangar that was our ballroom, or get an Eiffel tower cake bought for me in the interval, for the next few weeks.

The debates about allowing an American force in the Holy Loch continued for some time on current affairs programmes and my footage was always used. Nowadays one could expect to be a minor celebrity but in Scotland in those days, I was a show-off!

The Americans did arrive, many on the draft system, so there were Harvard and Yale men amongst them and very nice they were too. There were many Italian-American boys who recognised me as a 'Paisano' and suddenly, to be part Italian, was cool. They knew you weren't odd if you used olive oil in your food, and they certainly knew what spaghetti was, when in Dunoon at that time mushrooms were regarded with suspicion. There were many nationalities – Polish-American, Filipinos, German-American, Their ways were not our ways, but we learned to be cosmopolitan and accept this outgoing, free and easy people who seemed without a trace of self doubt.

My two friends were the first of a long line to marry Americans, and I was one of the few girls of my age group who did not go off to that far off land. Many people who, when young would not have thought to travel to Greenock, ended up crossing the Big Pond many times to visit their children. I still miss the Americans. □

soon after their generation's ordeal in World War II. They may secretly have felt grateful for the protesters but few of them would be prepared to join them. An ethos of conformity reigned strongly in small town Scotland.

Parallel to these feelings there was an anticipation of riches to be made from the business contracts and custom that may come to local businesses. They arrived at a time when things were changing rapidly for a small Scottish resort. There were great fears about their presence ruining Dunoon's holiday trade. In fact as we know now in retrospect that was going to face rapid decline in the sixties in any case as people travelled abroad more and more.

Local girl, Padye Girard dances with an American sailor

But once more The Safety Valve columns showed a conflict of expectations. A tourist wrote:

> May I, a Sassenach who has a great love for Scotland and its many beauties, add my protest to those which have already been made against the proposed use of the Holy Loch for an American missile-carrying submarine base? I speak only as one who has spent many pleasant hours at Dunoon, Kirn, Hunter's Quay and Holy Loch and the thought of this lovely little loch with its peaceful surroundings, its sailing craft bringing colour and beauty to its quiet waters becoming a base for United States war vessels, appals me. We are told that the crew of the Proteus will be 1100 and that about 400 members of their families will move to the Base. These women and children will need homes, shops, schools and other facilities if they are to be permanently established at or near the lochside. And if these good people are as 'car minded' as we are given to believe then presumably they will need garages, filling stations and car parking facilities. In other words Holy Loch and little towns which flank its shores will become commercialised.

Stalwart objectors continued to agitate in the pages of the local paper. Many of them lived around the shores of the Holy Loch and would be worst affected by this huge intrusion to its peaceful waters. There would be a mother ship, a dry dock and submarines coming in and out from patrol. The base would dominate the landscape and to many this was an abomination.

They were going to have to absorb the comings and goings of 1500 servicemen in their daily lives and look out on the military base on their beautiful loch, a truly shocking prospect. The constant noise of the Liberty boats would be inescapable, not to mention the noise of the industrial work on the dry-dock. They knew any radiation leaked from the Polaris missiles would affect them swiftly and inescapably. It was somehow obscene to think of this lovely, peaceful loch being silently polluted with an invisible, lethal killer. Some moved away with sadness.

A notice appeared in the *Standard* announcing 'the following petition to the Prime Minister is now open for signature at Mr Thomas's shop, Oakfield Place, Sandbank':

> To The Prime Minister, House of Commons.
> People of the Village of Sandbank, Holy Loch herewith protest vigorously against the setting up of a Polaris Submarine base in any part of Britain and call on the Government to urge the USA to stop the manufacture of this deadly new weapon. Saturation point in deterrents has long been passed and the magnitude of destructive power in the continuing Arms Race is creating a state of uncontrollable tension among the nations.

Morven Warren, (née Bell) was a teenager in 1961. She later married an American and settled in the USA

I do remember all the discussions about the impending arrival of the American Base, and the good and bad influence it might have on a small town like Dunoon. Despite that it seems like there was an air of excitement when they arrived.

I remember the afternoon the first ship docked at the Holy Loch as we lived on the West Bay and we could see crowds of sailors in uniform walking along the promenade. I remember one in particular strolling along with a girl on each arm.

Then of course we had the new American students at school. I remember being envious of their tans and those little pointed toe pumps the girls all wore (totally inadequate for our Scottish winters) and also the way they seemed to Americanise the school uniform. I didn't care for the crew cuts on the boys but the girls all seemed to have lovely hair and wore some make-up before we were allowed to wear it. Of course we all wanted to be friends with them.

I remember going to their homes and being amazed at how warm they were. I had never seen people walking around the house in short sleeves in the winter. We always seemed to have to layer on the woollen sweaters at home.

I thought they all did a great job of mixing in with us as it had to be so different from what they were accustomed to.

I hung around with a group of about 9 girls in school and 5 of us ended up married to Americans which is more than 50% so I would say the American Base had a huge impact on our lives. ❐

Over Here

The first day of the American arrival there was huge excitement as well as apprehension. After the disappointing sight of the *Proteus*, the streets were flooded with uniformed figures. Those first contacts were thrilling to children, akin to the first sightings of aliens.

They were very young and they were here. They wandered around town in their navy bellbottoms, neat tunics and pork pie hats. They charmed with their manners, calling women 'Ma'am' and men 'Sir'. They intrigued with their humour, they spoke in their loud voices. The American accent seemed so glamorous and the sailors attracted girls like magnets.

The national and international media of the day were in Dunoon in force, interviewing anyone willing to give their opinion. They filmed servicemen, arms around two girls at a time, strolling along Argyll Street, chewing gum, fulfilling every stereotype! Within a few days one had been invited to our home and a handsome film star could not have been afforded more attention. We stared at him in fascination, and laughed at his every joke. It must have been a disconcerting afternoon but his manners were impeccable.

The older people must have felt under siege. The phrase 'the Fleet's in' was never more true. The families were yet to arrive and so, this was our baptism in our new life.

Meanwhile the public relations had begun in earnest, with the ship's commanding officer, Captain Laning calling a press conference on board and speaking reassuring and conciliatory words about integrating and living in peace together.

Lady Provost CS McPhail was piped aboard the USS *Proteus* to meet him and Captain Ward, Commander of the 14th Submarine Squadron. She spoke warm words of welcome and said she hoped they would become fully integrated into the community. Then a civic reception was held for 150 officers and men in the Queen's Hall, Dunoon's landmark new building. Captain Ward said they were 'entranced by the beauty of the area and we are looking forward to living as part of the community. We have come because the government of the United Kingdom has asked us to be with you.' He said their mission was one of peace and nothing more. They wished to preserve it and their children would live with our children. They saw themselves as a stabilising factor. It was a gentle but sophisticated wooing.

People generally wanted to be reassured – it was too horrible to contemplate the other things they were hearing from anti-Polaris activists and some opposing experts. The local newspaper was the very important forum for the strong feelings expressed. The possible radiation exposure to children was one of the biggest issues. There were informative talks given by officers and wives, in various venues to calm fears about accidents. Why, they asked, would we put our own children in danger?

But there was no consensus. It was a divisive influence on Dunoon's local politics and society. There were arguments for and against, sometimes according to political views, sometimes according to business interests. Certainly the thought of prospering from this presence was inviting for many. It opened up possibilities for the future that were exciting, if you could set aside the fears. Scottish traditions of politeness and hospitality made us welcome the Americans. It would seem churlish to take our feelings out on individuals who had been ordered to come here as servicemen. We didn't want to give a bad impression.

Dunoon's Town Council of the day, whose members were of us and among us, gave civic receptions and polite speeches of welcome. The Americans responded with friendly overtures, and joined in with the annual calendar of local social events, such as the Fireman's Ball and Policeman's Ball, contributing some of their own such as the Officer's Ball, the Enlisted Men's Ball and the Chief Petty Officers' Ball. They took a high profile in public good works to present a benign face to us. They invited a local troupe of Highland dancers on to the *Proteus* to give a display to a full mess hall, with a feast afterwards. The *Proteus* chaplain gave talks to local Women's Guilds

They established the Polaris Cup yacht race to take

away any fears that sailing on the Loch would be ruined. Many of the Americans had Scottish ancestry and were thrilled to be in the mother country. They rushed to Edinburgh to soak up the atmosphere and loved the Cowal Highland Games as much as the locals. They attended Burns Suppers and attended the local churches with their families. They worked diplomatically to overcome local cynicism about their presence.

There was no infrastructure at the beginning – no housing, school or hospital or shop or sports facility. When they first arrived, families could stay in bed and breakfast for a limited number of weeks while they searched for a home in competition with hundreds of others. Local landladies were beginning to think about changing from holiday trade to accommodating American families on their arrival and departure. It was a quite different business. Holidaymakers were there for the spring and summer months and spent most of their time outdoors. The families were looking for a temporary home and would be spending a lot more time around the premises. Ways of working evolved. Landladies gave them the run of the kitchen to make their own food purchased from the commissary. They made bedrooms homely and child-friendly and loosened rules to make a relaxed atmosphere. There were good financial rewards and recommendations would bring more business.

'The Americans were much more relaxed as guests,' said a local ex-hotelier. 'They rarely complained even if they had to put up with less comforts than they were used to in our accommodation. They were polite and

Sandra Lumsden (née Cairns) was a schoolgirl when the American Base arrived

I clearly remember the night before the ship sailed in. There was a huge full moon and my sister said everything would be bigger and better because the Americans would be here soon. She was joking but I believed that life would be like the films, everyone would be glamorous and wearing fabulous clothes.

The first few weeks were quite dull, duffle coated people took part in CND marches, sailors in uniform were everywhere, the ship was grey, as were the submarines and the big cars looked out of place in our narrow streets. If the Americans didn't have a car they took a taxi, a practice soon to be copied by many of the locals. On the positive side our mothers just loved the charm of the sailors who would hold doors open and say, 'after you ma'am'.

As the weeks progressed the families arrived. My dreams of film star fashions were shattered. The majority of the Americans wore casual clothes, many casual to extreme with the women popping out to the shops in their curlers!

Their diet was extravagant by our standards – T-bone steaks, convenience foods purchased in their own commissary, mince was something they used to make burgers. Large barbeque grills were a standard item for those with even the smallest garden. We shared a love of bacon and eggs. However, the Americans ate bread and jam with their meal!

American women knew all about crafts whether it was quilting, patchwork, pottery or cake decorating. Craft clubs were popular in the town and formed a vehicle for the Scottish and American women to communicate. The two cultures got along well and appeared to have mutual respect for one another. I cannot remember any real problems.

In retrospect I think the real success story was the way the schoolchildren just got on with life. There was probably an American in every class. Initially this was a novelty. There was no special provision for the children, no fuss, no mention that they might be homesick and no special welcome. They were amazed by our school uniform but seemed to wear it with pride. However, they had slight variations, like bobby socks, (white slouch socks which we couldn't get!), button down collar shirts and brown penny loafers. They all seemed to have beautiful teeth and were not embarrassed to have worn a brace to correct defects. In class they were more outspoken than the Scots and confident about challenging teachers if they did not agree. Classes were lively, which must have been good for teachers and pupils.

When the servicemen finished their term of office the children went home to the States vowing to return some day. There was sadness but we would write and believed that some day we would meet up again.

I feel that the mix of cultures was good for both groups. I think the Americans did influence us to a certain extent, as I'm sure we influenced them. Children have the best of both worlds. Although we knew very well why the base was in Holy Loch we chose to ignore that and concentrated on what kids do well – accept and respect. ❑

"The US Navy had made no arrangements
to find housing with the result that many
of them could not find a place to stay"
Margaret Dalgaty

friendly and liked to share. Holidaymakers were upset if anything disappointed them on their annual fortnight.'

When one considers the size of the town and villages and around the base, it seems extraordinary that servicemen and their families were left to find their own accommodation. This was very difficult in the early days when locals had not yet realised the potential business opportunity opening up to them and were still taking ordinary holiday business in their boarding houses or flats. And then many had to make do with run-down homes and pay a premium rent for them. Some of the people making most of rental incomes were Glasgow people, descendants of the owners of the little holiday 'but n'bens'. Because single servicemen didn't want to live onboard the ship, they would pay high rents for a room and kitchen, some in squalid condition. The money was going out of town and any young couple looking for a home couldn't compete on rents. House sales were affected in that anyone who owned property in Dunoon would rent out rather than sell. It was a bonanza time for landlords, with demand far outstripping availability.

The officers did rather better as very soon the larger houses that had been built by Glasgow merchants for family holiday homes in Victorian times, quickly became available at large rents. People were responding to business and since no one knew how long this would last, they could hardly be blamed for making as much as possible on their property. Some of it was beautifully maintained and sought after. Some

was shamefully inadequate and yet the owners could profit greatly because of the shortage.

What was it like for Americans arriving in the early sixties, under our fierce scrutiny? They were so far ahead in the art of comfortable living. Central heating was a normality for most. Many of them came from States with hard winters but at home they sealed off their homes and turned up the heat, walking around in tee-shirts. They were startled to find that they had to rely on coal fires (they had to be taught how to build them) and electric heaters in these draughty old houses, with their tiny scullerys for cooking in, and wall larders for keeping perishables. They were allowed to ship their own furniture but where would the enormous fridge, washing machine and dryer fit in this arrangement?

They had to find ways to improve their situation quickly. As soon as a family moved into a rented house, it was carpeted wall to wall and the windows sealed with a plastic double glazing. Whatever form of heating there was would be turned up full and supplemented until it was stifling as far as we hardy Scots were concerned.

There was disbelief and disapproval at this way of living. To Scots people it was manifestly unhealthy to cut off all sources of fresh air! It was essential for children to get large doses of it no matter what the weather was like. It was common practice to put babies, new borns even, out in their prams in the garden to snooze in a layer of cosy blankets, winter and summer. Scots mothers thought it essential to take baby for long walks or shopping trips in all weathers. There was a widespread opinion that a lot of American babies looked pale and delicate because of their indoor life. The American mothers seemed to swaddle their babies and rush them from stifling home to car and back with as little exposure to the elements as possible. They seemed fearful of fresh air.

American fridges were huge and sturdy, beautifully designed with curved lines and easy-open doors. Opening that door made our eyes goggle. The shelves were stuffed with bottles of Coke, bologni, salami, steaks, ice cream in huge tempting tubs, American beer, ice by the bucket. The lowliest sailor seemed to live in a luxury of plenty. Their lives seemed dependent on their cars or taxis. They shipped their enormous cars over to Dunoon and chugged around our little streets in these fantasy Cadillacs and Chevrolets, with bench seats and enormous, power steering driving wheels.

Taxis multiplied to meet this sudden enormous demand. The quickest route from Dunoon to Ardnadam pier, where the Liberty boats to the ship plied back and forth, was over the High Road and down 'Lover's Lane'. A romantic place to stroll in the past, it became a treacherous race track. The route to the Bullwood, part of the road to Innellan, where the Officer's Club was situated, wasn't pleasant to walk either. Roads were narrow and unpaved then and the taxis and American cars would create rush hour conditions in these unlikely places. There were terrible accidents over the years, sometimes involving alcohol. Serious matters like these seem to disappear

Margaret Dalgaty was a young woman running a boarding house in Dunoon in 1961

The first families from the USA came to Dunoon at the height of the tourist season in July. Surprisingly the US Navy had made no arrangements to find housing with the result that many of them could not find a place to stay.

I had a small boarding house at that time and like many others was fully booked. Around 10pm a young mother came to my door, carrying a baby, a toddler by her side. She had walked all over the town and found no room at any inn. Her husband was on duty and was not allowed to meet her that day. I took the family in and let them stay the night on my dining room floor. The young mother had no change of clothing for the children, so I washed their clothes, made a meal and made a bed up on the floor. This was my first experience of the US Navy families.

Over the years I came to enjoy having these Americans stay, meeting many lovely people from all parts of the States. I also enjoyed the variety of the lives that they had.

Now and again I would have a family that was so different and unusual, that I would have to explain the simple rules of living here. One young woman from the Appalachian Mountains had brought a bucket to draw water and a shotgun to kill snakes. She walked around, all the time, in her bare feet. She hated wearing shoes. I had to explain that she ought not to go down town barefoot and it took a bit of persuading!

My husband and I had a very nice social life at that time with the US Navy, both with the families at our house and their friends. They came with us to the many balls and dances that went on in those days and we taught them to do the Scottish steps. In return we received invitations to the many American dances. ❐

John Forbes USN Nov. 1978 – August 1980 USS *Holland*. He now resides in Carmel, Indiana

It all began on Thanksgiving, back in November 1978. I had taken a commuter flight wearing my dress uniform and landed in Glasgow. I sat next to a man who shared the paper with me. I was nineteen years old, and thought of my lifelong dream of going back to Scotland, where a few short generations had me born in America, had just been realised. A black cab was waiting as I asked the man to take me to Queen Street Station, because I was a sailor bound for Holy Loch. He had a thick Glaswegian accent, and I felt a little embarrassed to ask him to repeat himself a few times. He was a very pleasant character, and asked why did I choose Scotland. I told him of my dream, and a broad smile crossed his face, and he said, I would do well here. All the while in the back of my head, it occurred to me I was relying on strangers to get me to Dunoon. I had no idea of Greenock, the Clyde Ferry, or Sandbank 55.982°N, 4.946°W, except from a brief brochure from my ship once I arrived!

I can still smell the train station, and look up through the roof to the crisp grey sky as if it were yesterday. As I boarded the train, a few curious stares passed my direction. During the trip I learned most sailors bound for Holy Loch didn't wear their uniform. I listened to the voices, watched the towns along the track, and every once in a while someone would say, 'so, you're bound for Holy Loch.'

I found out I had to take a boat to Dunoon, and found out that this was not my final destination. I purchased a ticket for the ferry and stood on the dock and looked over the Clyde. The sea air was cold for me, but invigorating, as the ferry let the cars and trucks off first, then the passengers. I saw Americans with Scottish girlfriends and families. I asked further directions from a sailor, and knowing I was a first hitch sailor, he grinned and told me where to find the taxi queue once I got to Dunoon. The ride on the Clyde was like a tour excursion for me. The sun was dipping lower, and I wondered if I would get to the ship before dark. I went and purchased a sausage roll and a tea, and watched over the rails, as the shoreline changed and we made for the dock. I looked for the Queen's Hall, and followed the road up Argyll Street. Never in my life did I see so many taxis! As I got in the driver said 'to the ship?' I had barely enough money left and another sailor stepped in to share the ride. The USS *Holland* (AS-32) – my ship and home till August 1980. I could barely contain my sense of excitement as I got out of the taxi. My companion for the ride pointed the way to the pier as was pulling my sea bag out of the boot. The MOD was a man without a speck of humour. He took me into his shack and went through my belongings, and sent me to the shack at the end of the pier.

I finished early my first day and was released two days to explore, and enjoy Scotland. I loved the town of Sandbank. I remember the bakery, with the cat in the window, fishmonger, chip shop, Crusader Pub/Disco, and Harmony Hotel. The ratio of women to men was in favour of the women, and there were fewer 'Dunoon Dolly's' than some made out to be. When I drank it was a wee dram of Grouse whisky, and a pint of Guinness stout.

What I remember most is the genuineness of the people. I felt such kinship with them. Sure there were a few that couldn't stand us Yanks. But for the most part, if you conducted yourself as a gentleman, and showed no snobbery, you made friendships that were true. My best Scottish friend, Tommy Doyle (he delivered coal by trade), helped me understand how to grow up, and what it means to be a true friend. My first love was in Scotland, and my first heartbreak too. I don't need to tell you of the depths of love and passion a Scottish woman can stir. She quoted Yeats.

For a short while I chanced to live in a home that Robert Burns had been in. It cost me a pint and fifty pounds a month, but it was home. Often I would stand close to the Highland Mary statue and dream of what it must have been like back when his love was alive.

One day, a few mates and I went ahead and started hill walking. If ever you have had the chance to climb and look out over Strathclyde, you have seen a vision of heaven. I have walked the deer trails through hillsides of clover so thick and full of fragrance that you have to experience it yourself, because there are no words to describe it.

I remember the coordinated events around the time of the Cowal Games; some sailors wore kilts of their own, or borrowed one from a local friend. I have one I purchased from a shop in Edinburgh. Nowadays, I have to lose some weight to fit it again. Because of my experiences at the Highland Games there, I look for them here. There is nothing like a good pipe band. While I favour the Royal Marines, we Yanks over the pond don't do a half bad job either.

I became a man in Scotland, land of my heritage. There is a portion of my heart left there. Scotland, and her people in reality were my first love, the one you never get over. ❐

The sound of the Liberty boats hummed late into the night, to some an irritant, to others a strangely comforting sound.

from view and the suspicion was that the American authorities had stepped in to deal with things discreetly in order to deflect the consequences. The sound of the Liberty boats hummed late into the night, to some an irritant, to others a strangely comforting sound.

It has been said in subsequent years that the first flush of personnel were carefully chosen to present a good impression to the apprehensive town. The American base sent to Scotland wasn't really a base at all, at the start. There was no complex of buildings and schools to absorb the service personnel so we were forced into each others' company. Great friendships developed.

But as Dunoon people were agog at their arrival, stories abounded in the early days of the strange ways of the 'Yanks'. Merging members of two societies would throw up the contrasts in national characteristics of each. Americans seemed to talk loudly and take over a room. They sounded as though they were bragging when they talked of home. Things were done differently and better in the States. This may have been the case, but it didn't seem polite to point it out to us so enthusiastically.

They were expansive and larger than life. If they lived next door they'd walk into your house without an invitation or a knock. They came from a huge, optimistic, confident country and it showed in their demeanor. Their ways weren't our ways but that didn't make them wrong or ill-mannered, they were just uncomplicated about being friendly.

Scotland did not have such healthy national pride then as now. We were a modest people and any emotional displays were embarrassing. It could be said we were rather buttoned up, or that we were dignified and reserved. We had to adjust to one another and be tolerant if we were going to cope with this enforced relationship.

As time went Dunoon people realised that the variation in background of servicemen was enormous. We started to distinguish between a rural one and a city one, a southern accent, and an east coast one, 'down-homey' and high-ranking (or both). We learned to distinguish between the Mid West and East and West Coast. We became more enlightened about the huge diversity of race and culture that constituted American society. Their physical characteristics and surnames could descend from Europe, the Far East, Africa or a wonderful mixture through intermarriage down the generations. We realised that many servicemen came from deprived backgrounds and had joined up to escape. Some of them talked of being unable to afford healthcare at home and we learned about the differences from our health service. In short, we became more sophisticated about treating them as individuals instead of lumping them all together as 'Yanks'.

America may be considered a classless society but there was as clear a hierarchy in its forces as there was in the British services. The officers were in careers and had a necessarily militaristic outlook. They wore, of course, peaked caps and braid on their jackets and carried briefcases. Their wives were elegantly dressed, in the emerging Jackie Kennedy style, and gracious in manner. They saw themselves as ambassadors for their country and had married into their husbands' careers. They devoted themselves to supporting him by running the family home as perfectly as possible. They had rank amongst the other wives according to their husband's position. They got involved in local charities, and were targets for the town's social climbers.

There were many annual dances in Dunoon in those days, very dressy affairs, and these couples attended as many as they could, as a way of integrating with the local business people. They were conservative in manner and eager to make a good impression. We rarely saw them out shopping in rollers and head-scarves, as we often did some of the ordinary servicemen's wives. As Britain was still quite formal in dress in those days, this was often commented on, in shocked voices. It was just different. Women had to style their hair with rollers and lacquer, then. Their lives revolved around their husbands and they wanted to look their best when they drove the station wagon to pick him up from work. It was all part of their relaxed daytime style for taking care of the house and family.

Fairly quickly a shopping facility for American goods and liquor was set up, called the Commissary, an Officers' Club and an Enlisted Men's Club, at Ardnadam. 'These facilities helped relieve the excessive naval presence in a small town. The occasional obnoxious behaviour by drunken sailors was then mostly confined to the EM Club rather than in the Argyll or Crown Hotels in Dunoon,' says retired Captain Art Bivens, in his book *From Nukes to Nosecones*.

Permission: Jim Collins

US Navy man Jim Collins at the Enlisted Men's Club (formerly Ardnadam Hotel) in 1964

The US Navy made great efforts formally to integrate. Many social events were organised and clubs and societies encouraged

(Above) Kirn Scouts take part in a visit aboard USS *Hunley* in 1965

(Right) Councillor William Hunter, Chairman of Argyll & Bute Council presenting a quaich to Captain Ronald Gumber t Jnr, USN Commander Submarine Squadron 14, with Admiral Jeremy Boorda, USN Commander in Chief, US Naval Forces Europe. This took place at the ceremony in 1992 to mark the closure of the base, but such official good relations typified the mood between the US forces and community representatives

© Herald & Evening Times (NEWSQUEST) Ltd

Permission: Gordon Trapp

Magistrate and Dunoon Provost Gordon Trapp has done a quick change from his telephone engineer duties to be on hand to welcome Captain George Ellis of the USS *Simon Lake* in 1966

Gordon Trapp, former Provost of Dunoon

When the USS *Proteus* first sailed up the Clyde past Dunoon, the promenade was lined with local residents and the CND gathered at the Argyll Gardens to march in protest to Ardnadam Pier. As the *Proteus* sailed into the Holy Loch canoes and other small craft did everything possible to hamper events. The MOD police were well-prepared for the disruptions at sea. The Argyll constabulary was in force at the head of Ardnadam Pier to deal with any trouble there. A certain amount of trouble took place both on land and sea, but the main protesters were apprehended and held in a hall adjacent to the sheriff court.

As a British Telecom technical officer I was assigned to connect landline communications to the *Proteus* – underwater cables had been laid in preparation from the Anchorage buoy to the MOD police hut at the head of the Pier. At 8 am I was stationed ready to make these connections, but told, under no circumstances was I to leave until the land lines were connected. I was given a hand-held radio to contact my American equal. It was well into the afternoon before I heard a voice on the radio asking what I wanted done. Connecting with the ship's wiring took the rest of the afternoon. Try as I might I could not get him to understand how I wanted him to pair up the 32 cores in the cable. As it was now getting on for 9 pm I reported the troubles to a supervising officer who told me permission had been made for me to go on board to sort things out. I made all connections at the Shore end and a boat was sent to take me out to the *Proteus*. I was introduced to a young second-class I/C sailor who was to be my escort. This lad, Tom

Kenney, soon learned British Telecom expressions and by 3 am the following morning we had full landline communications established. On each occasion I had to go on board again I was met by Tom and we became good friends, I invited him home to meet my wife and family. He and our son, Ian, became buddies and he spent all his shore leave at our home. Many more homes were opened up to the US Navy men as they were welcomed by the town's folk.

As the senior magistrate and provost of Dunoon from 1965 to 1968 I had many dealings with the senior brass of the US Navy. One amusing occasion was when the USS *Simon Lake* was relieving the USS *Hunley* and I, as a telephone engineer had to change the shoreline cables from one ship to the other. There I was sitting on the cable buoy preparing the cables when the *Simon Lake* was passing Ailsa Craig. I as provost of the town was to welcome the ship's crew to Scotland so I had to down tools and board the boat which took me to Ardnadam Pier where I hurriedly changed from overalls to kilt and chain of office and along with Commodore Woodall I sailed out to meet the *Simon Lake* off Innellan before she entered the Holy Loch. We were welcomed a board by Captain George Ellis. The ship then continued to the Holy Loch where I went ashore and changed back into overalls picked up my tools and back to the *Simon Lake* to complete the changeover. When I arrived back on the *Simon Lake* the officer of the watch looked at me in dismay, but, I soon explained my dual duties.

Many other times my dual appearances caused wonderment, especially when US personnel appeared in court and I was the presiding magistrate. ◻

The *Los Alamos* dry dock about to be loaded onto the ship taking it back to the States at the closure of the base in 1992

Permission: Gordon Trapp

Permission: Del Porchetta

Social events took place between Scots and American communities

(top) Provost Gordon Trapp (rt) at an anniversary dinner in Washington DC of the Armed Services YMCA

(bottom) Del and Margaret Porchetta (left on each row) at an American Ball with other Royal Navy and showbiz guests

Del Porchetta

From 1971 my wife Margaret and I (I was handyman/gardener) ran a B&B which gradually became popular with arriving and departing families from Subron 14 of the US Navy. As many of these families ended up staying with us for as long as two months we tried to make it home from home for them and developed many lasting friendships. (Dr Laurel Salton the ill-fated US astronaut lodged with us on her first arrival in Scotland.)

Over the years the formality of the dining room disappeared and everyone breakfasted in our large farmhouse kitchen which also became the venue for many parties. Many a guest was introduced to the delights of Scotch whisky during winter evenings spent in the kitchen over games of Probe and Pictionary. Indeed our social life was quite hectic in these days. We received many invitations to the annual Balls held by the various squadron ranks, and lavish and entertaining events they proved to be.

As a keen yachtsman I crewed on my friend Ian Mitchell's yacht in many Polaris Regattas which were jointly sponsored by the Holy Loch Sailing Club and the US Navy. Again the shore-side activities at these events were superb with lashings of food and drink followed by a prize-giving and dance.

Our eldest son married an American girl and now lives in a large farmhouse in Maine. As a result we now have three wonderful American grandchildren who love visiting Scotland. Since the closure of the Base in 1992 we have had return visits from many former serving personnel, and we in turn feel we could travel coast to coast in the US just staying with friends. ❐

"we could travel coast to coast in the US just staying with friends"

Greta Yorke (née Beggs)

My first memory of the American arrival in Dunoon was of being at church one Sunday. Some of the sailors had come to the service. The minister welcomed them and asked the congregation to welcome them to their homes and offer them some hospitality. Now, by chance my mother's cousin's baby was being baptised that Sunday and we were all going to the reception after the service. As we made our way out of the church it was apparent to my parents that the only sailors left alone were two black lads. You have to understand black people were a bit of a novelty in Dunoon at that time!

My dad told my mum to invite them to the reception after the service. She was a little concerned about arriving with two American sailors but she asked them along and introduced them to everyone. They were made welcome and these two young men, George and Sam, remained family friends throughout their tour of duty. ❐

At Christmas the ship and the dry dock,
those sinister symbols of war, were
decked in spectacular lights and messages
of good will to all men

Strikingly we found out just what a generous people Americans are. Their casual hospitality drew us into their social lives and introduced us to their plentiful, cheap liquor in the form of Southern Comfort, Jack Daniels and Harvey Wallbangers. People found out the hard way how generous the American drinks measures were in those large glasses. We developed a taste for fizzy American beer from the fridge. We ate their pasta, pizzas, pretzels, their hot dogs and hamburgers. Betty Crocker cake mixes and muffin mixes offered us the lazy way to bake. Crisco, a glutinous pure white fat from a tin was a mainstay of the delicious cookies they rustled up. Their children grew tall on copious amounts of milk and cheese.

Our mothers must have looked on in envy, especially as we children loved to eat in American homes. We babysat, taking up their offers to help ourselves to cokes and sandwiches from the giant fridge and earned unheard of sums of money to spend in Mr Begbie's or Gibson's, the only places to buy the current Top Twenty records. We listened to their music collections. (I first heard black soul music while late night babysitting for the black family next door to us). We enjoyed their wonderful extravagant magical Christmas light displays, that still inspire Dunoon residents to this day. The ship and the dry dock too, those sinister symbols of war, were decked in spectacular lights and messages of good will to all men. To some the irony was not lost!

Living together meant intermarriage between many Scots women and US servicemen.

In the years following the arrival of the base, an annual average of 40 marriages are recorded by Cowal Registrars as having taken place between partners of different nationality. It is difficult to trace but there is every reason to believe at least the same number of such weddings took place elsewhere including in the USA

Living Together

The differences between Scotland and America showed up most at school, where local children and the offspring of sevice personnel were thrown together. At Dunoon Grammar School some of the older teachers had grown up with Victorian parents and lived through two world wars. Most of the men had served in the war or had done National Service and they had great gravitas. A few had terrifying reputations that went before them as they strode along the ancient corridors, their black teachers' gowns flowing. Gilbert McAllister, (English) George Galt, (Latin) Archie Blair, (English and History) Roland Singer, (French) and headmaster, AE Smith, were among those who dominated the academic landscape of the time.

These teachers had booming voices and erudite vocabularies to express their contempt for any pupil failing to meet their high expectations. Joe Dallas reigned supreme in Gym and Sports for the boys, while Miss Mar (nicknamed Minnie) maintained a strict regime in PE for the girls. Miss Campbell and Miss Taylor were a formidable presence in English and French, respectively. Gentle Mr Cameron ran the music department, Mr Cannon, Geography and Mr McCartney the Art Department. The belt was a legal form of punishment and some of them used it freely, men and women. There were very strict rules of behaviour instilled in us from an early age.

American children walked into our classrooms in the early days like innocent lambs. Their confidence sometimes extended to expressing opinions freely and loudly during lessons and challenging what the teacher was saying. This was obviously encouraged in American schools as a healthy way of learning. In Dunoon Grammar School it was sometimes regarded as an impertinent behaviour and bewildered children were punished accordingly.

A few younger teachers made allowances and even began to encourage discussion. Far from being impertinent most of these children had perfect manners and had to show respect to their parents in ways that astonished us. Officers' kids often had to call their father 'sir' and live with strict rules at home. This sometimes resulted in a wildness out of the home, which some locals felt was a bad influence on their children.

We'd never seen 'slam books' before – a form of cruel and unusual punishment unless you were Mr Handsome or Miss Popularity. Names were written at the top of a page in a blank jotter and it was passed around for others to write comments about each victim. As it could be done anonymously it was often irresistable if soul-destroying to look at your page.

American teen magazines were passed around, whose sexy stories left our *Bunty*, *Judy* and *Romeo* far behind. Another minefield was the issue of make-up. American girls seemed to have a sophistication about them that was encouraged in their society and wore make-up at an earlier age. What's more, they wore it to school and this was a shocking thing to do in the eyes of older women teachers. Long lectures about modesty ensued and appropriate behaviour for young ladies was explained by Miss M in a terse voice.

The most revolutionary element of all was the freely expressed interest by the girls in the opposite sex. Scottish girls had no less an interest, but any obvious pursuit of it was called 'wearing your heart on your sleeve' and strongly discouraged by teachers (a nod to Victoria here). We had a visiting tutor in Sex Education. Miss D was large and elderly and, unwittingly, the cause of much hilarity, though lord help you if she caught you laughing. She tackled her subject with great enthusiasm and so directly that frissons of shock ran through the hall, already tensed with dread. She seemed a relic of a long ago age, the age of 'hygiene and purity' and was far from being a role model for us.

The modern attitudes of the American pupils were bringing a timely breath of fresh air into the stuffy old corridors. As Marian Dawes (née Paton) recalls, 'Miss D's annual classes wouldn't have been as much fun without the input from the American girls!'

Altogether these American children seemed so worldly amongst us. Most of them had lived in many different places and had developed social skills to cope with these changes. The girls seemed so perfectly groomed and poised. In school they had to adjust to wearing uniform. Out of school, they wore fine sweaters, nylons or bobby socks, loafers and plaid skirts. They were called names like Bonnie or Cindy or Candy. They had strange, long, foreign-sounding surnames. Their hair was always styled and shiny. They wore American perfumes and ate Hershey bars. They carried their piled-up schoolbooks, no schoolbags. The boys wore crew cuts and had a handsome look with their casual elegance, loafers and fine sweaters. They were called Brad or Rick or Junior. Their attractiveness added an element of excitement to schooldays and it wasn't long before boy/girl relationships began between Scots and Americans. Some of these romances ended in marriage.

A Scottish newspaper reporter of the time wrote:

With pride, 45 American children wear the uniform of Dunoon Grammar School. With gratitude, their parents enrol them in an old school which believes the way to educate children is to give them lots of hard work and discipline. The opportunity to have their families educated under the Scottish school system is one reason why a posting to the USS Hunley is so popular with married men. But nothing in Dunoon Grammar School resembles schooling in America. The Rector of Dunoon Grammar is Alexander Smith, a graduate of Aberdeen University, who has spent his entire teaching life at the Grammar. He makes no concessions for the 45 Americans among the 750 Scottish children. He is a dominie of the old school. His American pupils interest him and there is nothing which escapes his notice.

The first group of American pupils pose with A. E. Smith, the headmaster of Dunoon Grammar School

The PSI SIGMA CHI youth club, with Scots and American members.

(Front) Wendy Allan, Bobby Wright, Betsy Messersmith, Clara Kicklighter, Glen Anders

(Middle) Lynn Wannamaker, Diane Yarbrough, Candy Clifford, Nancy Boyd, Midge Parlata, Sherri Nisonger, Eileen McCartney, Sharon Gauger, Joy Teague

(Back) Niall Stirling, Melinda Digg, Merry Straus, Stevie Cushman, George Johnstone, Kathy Kephart, Alastair Ross, Gwen Boyd, Ross MacLeod, Donna Cushman, Iain Stirling

Contacts from youth events in the 1960s

Teen Club Members October 1964

ADAMS Tom, Promonado House, East Bay
BROWN Eric, Waterside, Glenmorag Crescent
BURGESS Norma, 1 Allan Terrace, Sandbank
CARUTHERS Debbie, Gowan Bank, Clyde Street
CARUTHERS Paul, Gowan Bank, Clyde Street
CLIFFORD Candy, Ardengrove, Sandbank
COFFMAN Brenda, Gowanlea, Wellington Street
COLQUHOUN Wallace, Pearl Cliff, Hill Street
CUSHMAN Donna, The Grange, Hunter St, Kirn
CUSHMAN Stevie, The Grange, Hunter St, Kirn
DALLAS Rab, Ardblair, Hunter's Quay
EMERY Christine, Ivy Grove, Cromwell Street
GILLIES John, 37 Dixon Avenue, Kirn
GLIDEWELL Sam, Edenkyle, West Bay
GOW Alister, 38 Ardenslate Crescent, Kirn
HUNT Janet, Trentino, Sandbank
HUTCHERSON Casey, Dunmore Hotel, Kirn
JOHNSTONE George, Dunloskin Farm
KNOX John, 20 Cowal Place
McGARVIE Charles Ashton View, Alfred Street
MacEWAN Alan, Woodside, Mary Street
MacEWAN Alister, Woodside, Mary Street
McLEOD Alan, Waterworks House
MESSERSMITH Betsy, Marshill, Kilbride Road
MESSERSMITH Ralph, Marshill, Kilbride Road
MITCHELL Robert, 105 Eward Street
PITT Jimmy, 64 Auchamore Road
PRIEST Robert, Birchfield, Hunter's Quay
PRIEST Valerie, Birchfield, Hunter's Quay
REID Tommy, Healthfield, King Street
ROSS Alastair, Wentworth, Park Avenue
SALMON Rebecca, Kilmory, Bullwood
SAYLES Paul, Benruthven, Hunter Street
SISSON Annette, Mount Melville, Stewart St, Kirn
SISSON Laura, Mount Melville, Stewart St, Kirn
STIRLING Alex, 1 Miller Terrace
STIRLING Iain, Craigower, Auchamore Road
STIRLING Niall, Craigower, Auchamore Road
SMITH John, 42 Ardenslate Crescent, Kirn
TEAGUE Joy, Eastwood, King Street
THOMAS Eileen, 143 George Street
THOMPSON Tim, Benthead Sandbank
WADDEL Alan, 31 Cowal Place
WADE Denis, Helenslea, Jane Street
WALTON George, Montn Melville, Seweart St, Kirn
WANNAMAKER Lynn, Rosevale, Kilbride Road
WHITE Kathy, Jasmine, Pilot Street
WILLIAMS David, Cloch View, Alexander Street
YOUNG Libby, 3 Queen's Road, Sandbank

They appear to be more sophisticated but their apparent maturity is superficial. They are less inhibited but are very well mannered. They are more articulate – quicker and more confident in expressing themselves.

Stephanie Barrett, a lovely 16-year old who wears a Campbell tartan kilt says, 'School in Scotland is completely different to America. In the States pupils are drilled to ask questions, hold and express different views to their teachers, discuss every subject. Teacher is a chum of the pupil.'

Candy Syverson, a delightful 16 year old, says she loves school in Scotland. And she knows how much benefit she is getting from a Scottish education. Both girls want to join the Peace Corp. They both want to learn Russian. They have no settled home which means that the world is their university. And no one except their parents appreciates more the opportunity to learn under a system which has an unparalleled world reputation.

A teenage social club was set up, run and chaperoned by American parents. It was called Psi Sigma Chi and was connected to the YMCA established for servicemen. It ran dances and socials and outings. When the Beatles era began it was exciting for American teenagers to go to Glasgow and see the British groups of the time. Dunoon youngsters became connected to the American calendar of events, being invited to celebrate the 4th of July at a public picnic at Loch Striven every year, with a spectacular firework display to follow, from the coal pier in Dunoon's West Bay. We became aware of Thanksgiving's importance in American family life. We went to all night 'pyjama parties'! We tuned to Radio Caroline and listened to the Beachboys, the Supremes and Tamla Motown. The Americans loved our folk music and got involved with our politics when we had a mock election at school. They went on school trips to Europe. We were introduced to 'Record Hops'. Those formative teenage years when we absorb so much, were enriched for all of us by the new elements introduced by the integration.

One of the less pleasant social consequences of having a military base full of young, single men with dollars to spend was the arrival of prostitutes from all the nearby cities.

They seemed to know when a submarine came back from patrol and in a small town were extremely conspicuous, not least because of their mode of dress. There was no subtlety in their approach, as time meant money to these business women (and many were older women). They wore their hair piled high and fiercely lacquered. Their make-up heavy and striking, they tottered on tall stilleto heels and clutched cheap fur coats around their thin dresses. It was an attempt at a poverty-based glamour that announced their availability for business, directly and in time-honoured tradition. Of course they stood out like beacons of immorality, brazenly carrying out their trade in front of mortified locals. It brought about a revulsion when

stories were passed around about the inevitable sights that were seen in various quiet spots, of which there were plenty around the district.

The Scottish newspapers were always looking for stories and the sleazier the better. We were growing up in 'little America' and a 'vice town'. It was highly insulting to decent Americans as well. But there was an inevitable dramatic rise in 'immoral behaviour' and the newspapers loved it as a source of stories when things were quiet on other fronts.

The number of illegitimate births had quadrupled in the first year of the base's presence. In those times, this was considered a true sign of moral decay. The local newspaper's letters column was bombarded in these early days as people had to come to terms with this new unpleasant reality.

> I am sick of reading articles in magazines and newspapers about Dunoon and I am sure many other people are too.
>
> As for an article this week in a magazine, people in other towns and cities will think it is nothing but prostitutes who walk about the streets of our town.
>
> The council say they have tried to stop vice coming into Dunoon. I agree it is a hard thing to do, but after reading this article (and don't forget people all over the country will have read it too) don't you think further steps should be taken to, as the Americans say, clean this town up.

I am just one of the many girls very angry after reading this article and am not interested in American sailors.

The editor inserted a statement in response to this:

This matter was discussed in private by Dunoon Town Council on Tuesday night. Among other proposals it was suggested that the Commander of the ship be asked to impose a 12 o'clock curfew on single navymen to be aboard at that hour and that the Chief Constable of Argyll be asked to increase the number of Constables on duty in Dunoon and tighten up on the night adventures of the Americans. The agreement between Mr Macmillan and Mr Kennedy to use Polaris submarines in the Holy Loch has never been formally ratified by the House of Commons. It should be ended now. Ed.

Such views intermingled with the resentment of the American presence. In the early days, it brought about a prejudice towards perfectly innocent girls who went out with an American boyfriend and towards sailors who would never behave badly. There was trouble between local men and sailors when they got too close to one another in pubs and competed for women. The uniforms acted as a provocation in these situations and later, it was forbidden to wear it ashore.

Also within the servicemens' own community there could be trouble between submariners (nicknamed 'bubbleheads') and sailors ('seaskimmers'). The submarines would return after weeks at sea and the crew would hit the town, maybe provoking trouble with their exuberance.

An 11'o clock curfew was imposed on the sailors by Commander Laning for a while to stop this situation escalating. Gradually hotels and pubs made a choice about who they wished to encourage, the dollar crowd or the locals and holidaymakers. And everyone knew which was which.

There was an underlying feeling in the early days that a girl chose between Americans or local boys to date. If you chose American you went to American parties and socials and cut yourself off from your Dunoon peer group to an extent. Americans would turn up at local dances, young men out for a good time, ask girls to dance and immediately trouble would start. It was the most natural thing in the world for young people to see attraction in 'otherness' and to ignore all the undercurrents and raging prejudices that wanted to prevent these new relationships.

The tensions that these young sailors had to cope with must have been great. But their great success with girls, because of their charm and easy manner, and their determination to enjoy every minute of leave, put them at odds with the community. They were accused of 'babysnatching' teenagers – though some were just teenagers themselves.

A national newspaper ran an article about a deputation to the *Proteus* Captain, calling for this under-age dating to stop but the American authorities didn't seem to take this as seriously as expected. An American wife was contemptuous and in a letter to the Safety Valve suggested that a curfew be imposed on the young girls of the town, if their parents felt so worried. In an angry reply a local parent fumed:

> An American wife may think us prudish, old-fashioned or what she likes but for a foreigner to tell us what to do is another matter. Why should Scottish girls have their liberty curtailed simply because American sailors have not the good manners to conform to the customs of a country in which they temporarily find themselves? Our girls normally mix with their contemporaries, with whom they have grown up and who are known to their families.
>
> Disgruntled Americans would do well to remember that Scottish upbringing and education differ substantially from their own, and that such a document as the Kinsey Report is unlikely to make us feel that their methods produce results we would like to see in this country.

Local young men were bound to resent this constant challenge in uniform, so unabashed and outgoing, as most of them were. Everyone was hyped up for these encounters and it didn't take much for fights to start. One American wife, resentful of the tirades in the local press, retaliated with her own views:

After two years of reading about overpaid, missile-mad, big car-addicted, young girl-chasing Americans, I think it is high time you published an American's idea on some of Dunoon's folks. You people have feelings, so do I, so please print my entry.

Local thought – Americans are highly paid! My reply – we had better be, when some of the landlords charge us £35 a month rent, when to locals it would be £5 a month.

Local thought – Polaris will blow us all to bits or cause the Russians to do it! My reply – What happened during the Cuba crisis? Didn't the Proteus move out completely? No target left. Russians won't waste a missile or anything else in Dunoon.

Local thought – Americans are big car-addicted. My reply – We worked and paid for them. One of your leading citizens drives a Cadillac.

Local thought – American sailors are ruining our young girls' morals. My reply – Your young girls are ruining our sailors' morals. From what I've seen, to put it mildly, they are more ready, willing and able. The way they are painted up, you can't tell whether they are 13 or 30. They don't seem to care whether the man is married or single. Just as long as he's a 'Yank'.

Local thought – Americans shouldn't be allowed duty free purchase of tobacco, spirits, etc, etc.
My reply – Your own British Navy and their dependents enjoy this privilege. Why be jealous of Americans?

Local thought – Americans are far too noisy.
My reply – Americans by admission are outgoing, friendly, gregarious and talkative individuals, and if we can't conform to your standards we apologise. However, we will continue to be the same friendly, helpful folks as always.

Local thought – If you don't like our ways, go back to America!
My reply – Thanks, I will. Am leaving very shortly. And as I'll look back over the hills of Argyll I can honestly say, you folks would be treated differently in our country. (Same rent for Scots as Americans)

For two years I tried to ignore the sarcasm, printed in the paper about us Americans, but my red American blood is boiling. So 'Cheerio, lang may your lum reek!'

The Sheriff Court was dealing with a lot more customers and the local police were under some strain. However the American Shore Patrol worked alongside them to keep things under control.

On landing personnel came into the jurisdiction of Customs and Excise, under the aegis of the Ministry of Defence. They were landing on a foreign country every time they left the Liberty boats and could be searched for contraband material, ie anything beyond their tobacco allowance or illegal substances. The Shore Patrol was headed by a Chief Petty Officer and staffed by around eight temporary personnel supplied by different divisions on board the supply ship and one person per night from any visiting submarine. Patrols were also sent to Glasgow and Greenock to dance halls frequented by sailors. These helmeted enforcers carried night sticks and travelled in large military wagons, designed for transporting any 'sinners'. They only had powers over American military personnel and in the early days patrolled with the local police force, who had jurisdiction over everyone.

On board ship the Master-at-Arms was the policing authority and American marines were responsible for security, a matter taken very seriously, considering the weaponry on board for supply to submarines. The captain would decide the fitting punishment for any serviceman who had transgressed military regulations, such as going AWOL or trying to smuggle alcohol aboard. In the early days being sent to the Brig meant a diet of bread and water. It could mean a session hammering rocks around Ardnadam Pier, with sailor

The American Years

"We don't object to you. Ye're here
because you have a job to do. It's yer
bliddy government that sent the bombs."
Elderly Dunoon resident
buying a US serviceman a pint

hat worn in a certain way, brim pulled down, in full
view of shipmates passing, for full humiliation.

Sailors soon found their way to Glasgow and
Edinburgh for weekend leave. The pubs in Dunoon
closed at 10 o'clock in those days and there was little
else to do until the complex was built to provide
services and leisure activities, such as a bowling alley,
for sailors. A hamburger stand had appeared at the pier
where sailors disembarked from liberty boats. (Later
teenagers would often end a night out there if they
were lucky enough to have a car.)

Romances blossomed and marriages followed. At
the end of the *Proteus* tour of duty, an American
newspaper article headlined '130 Sailors found wives
in Scotland' read 'I love a lassie, a bonny Highland
lassie – This is the theme song of 130 crew members of
the *Proteus* which arrived in Charleston yesterday, for
they all married Scottish girls during their two year stay
in Holy Loch.' A sailor explained why so many *Proteus*
men had lost their hearts to Scots girls: 'They're . . .
well . . . very attractive, and not so difficult to please as
the girls over here. They were always a pleasure to
date, didn't want to head for the bright lights but were
happy just being in your company.' The sailor had met
his bride at a *Proteus* dance. 'Dances are very popular
over there and they gave the boys a chance of meeting
the local girls.'

A sailor explained why
so many Proteus men had lost their hearts
to Scots girls:
'They're . . . well . . . very attractive'

Tom Barbour

My first visit to a pub, in Dunoon, I asked for a beer, and I didn't know the difference between lager, heavy and an elderly gentleman told me to have a pint of heavy, and when I went to pay, he bought me the drink.

He then told me that he didn't want American weapons in the Holy Loch, but 'we don't object to you. Ye're here because you have a job to do. It's yer bliddy government that sent the bombs here.'

I was on the *Proteus* when we came to the Holy Loch on February 22, 1961. On the morning of our arrival, I walked out on the port side weather deck as *Proteus* was cruising south in the Irish Sea toward the Firth of Clyde, just a mile or two off the coast of Scotland. The day was heavily overcast and grey, but there was a small break in the clouds that let one beam of sunshine through to a field on the hillside, and lit it the brightest green I had ever seen. I remember realising that, no matter how different things were to me in this foreign land, there was a great deal of beauty to be found.

Three months later, a large group of mostly outsiders came to Dunoon to protest the American presence in the Holy Loch. One of their leaders was Rev James Curry, of St James Church of Scotland in Glasgow, and one of his parishioners was Irene Harrison, a raven-haired beauty from Pollok.

Rev Currie married us in his church the following March, and this past March 2003 we celebrated forty-one years of marriage.

A Glasgow newspaper photographer came with a reporter, who put an article in the paper about us. We had planned a big wedding in June, and then the Navy came out in February with an edict that they would not 'authorise' any dependents on station unless the serviceman was going to be there a year. Since my enlistment was up the following March 29, I had just a little more than a year to go then, but I'd only have nine months remaining in June. If dependents were not authorised, we wouldn't get the housing allowance (about $90 a month in 1962), shipment of household goods, and dependents' transportation to the US. I questioned the edict, and asked about servicemen who acquired a dependent when he had less than a year to go. The Executive Officer, a really fine gentleman, checked with the Navy Command in London. He told me, sympathetically, that the ruling was that if I had less than a year remaining on station when I got married, my wife would not be authorised to be there. I guess I sort of lost it.

'What the hell do they mean she wouldn't be authorised to be here? She was born here! She's a British subject! She's got more (expletive deleted) right to be here than you do!'

So we quickly moved our plans ahead, to March 10, and the paper printed a big story about us on our wedding day. Before we returned from our honeymoon, the Navy said the ruling had been misinterpreted, and that we could have waited until June and Irene would have been authorised to be there. □

American Tom Barbour and local girl Irene Harrison 'a raven-haired beauty from Pollock' met when Irene was demonstrating against the base

Linda Pursley (née Jones) was a young woman living with her parents in the Laudervale Hotel, in Dunoon, when the Base arrived

First of all we were assured that the sailors would be confined to their depot ship, the USS *Proteus* and they would very rarely be seen in town! My father was taking no chances. When I asked if I could go out and see the ship's arrival I was given an emphatic no. When I asked why, he said he had been in the British army himself during the war and he 'knew what young men get up to when they are in uniform!' I was 17 years old and promptly confined to my room.

As time went by and the CND protest marchers had made their statement and gone home, the sailors were allowed off the ship for R&R when they were off-duty.

I met one particular sailor named Henry [Hank] Long, and went out with him for a while, much to my father's annoyance. I tried to get the two of them to meet once, but Hank chickened out at the last-minute when he saw the look on my father's face and promptly drove out of our driveway at great speed! Ironically, I am still in touch with Hank and his wife and we correspond regularly by e-mail.

The first thing most of the local girls noticed about the American boys was their politeness. If they ask you out, they always offered to come to your house and take you to the dance, paying your way in. The Scottish boys on the other hand, would say that they would meet you in the dance, meaning that they didn't have to pay!

One of the first things many of the sailors did was buy a second hand car to get around in. This was at a time in Scotland when many families weren't financially able to own a car, and made a great impression on the girls, much to the annoyance of the local lads, who weren't earning anywhere near the same salaries as the Americans and certainly couldn't afford a car. On the other side of the coin, many of the sailors said how nice it was to meet a Scottish girl whose first question wasn't 'what kind of a car do you drive' as they did in the US. We didn't expect our boyfriends to have cars. Another thing we noticed was how clean they were and how good they smelled. This was at a time in Scotland when many houses still did not have proper bathrooms, and many Scottish men were lucky to have a bath once a week, never mind daily as did most of the Americans.

I met Gerry in June 1962 at a dance in the Dunoon Pavilion. I went with a girlfriend, and saw him sitting on his own on the other side of the room. It was love at first sight – for me anyway! I walked over and asked him for a dance and he said no – as he didn't know how to dance. At that point, I wished the floor would open up and swallow me.

But as I had already determined that he was 'the one', I sat down beside him and we started chatting. He walked me home and we started seeing each other regularly until the Cuban crisis in October of that year, when the ship had to leave with only 20 minutes notice, taking him with it. I didn't know where they had gone and whether they would ever be back, but after 10 long days which felt like years, the ship returned and we were engaged two days later. We married on Valentine's Day 1963 and returned to the States in September 1964, by which time we had one daughter and another on the way.

When we returned to Dunoon in August 1971, things were very different. The Navy had been here for eight years by then and the

US Navy man Gerry Pursley and local girl Linda Jones marry in 1963

sailors and their families had become almost totally integrated into the local community. By then they had a Commissary and Navy Exchange where they purchased most of their groceries, clothes and other items, but those things which they couldn't buy in there, they usually bought locally, bringing great benefit to the local shops, pubs and taxi businesses. There was no Navy housing until the mid '70s, so they also lived in the local community and their children went to the local schools making friends with the local children. Many also joined local groups such as country dancing, the golf club, etc. and several American girls learned Highland dancing. I think these were the best years, although it has to be said that due to an acute shortage of housing, many service personnel were forced to live in very substandard accommodation. A few young wives commented that it was like stepping back in time 30 or 40 years and most had never even seen a coal fire before, let alone have to use it as their main source of heating! It was no wonder that they welcomed the newly built Navy housing with open arms.

However, when most of the families began to live in the newly built Navy communities, some of the closeness between the Navy community and the local community began to diminish, with some Navy families leaving after two or three years, having never met any local families. As more recreational facilities were built for the Americans, which the locals were unable to use, there was some resentment, especially when it came to things like the very cheap prices which the Americans were paying for alcohol, cigarettes and petrol, compared to British prices. This was not the fault of the American community, but of our British Customs and Excise, but many locals didn't see things that way.

Two of the highlights of the social calendar during the last 20 years of the US Navy's presence was the Site One Ball and the Christmas Tea. The first one was held in the Queen's Hall and many locals who were either married to Americans or who had American friends were invited to attend. They were wonderful occasions and great fun. The Christmas Tea was hosted by the wife of the Commodore in her home at Ardbeg, Kilmun. The local ladies competed frantically for an invitation to attend this annual event, and oohed and aahed at the beautiful handmade Christmas decorations, the dozens of poinsettias dotted throughout the house and the wonderful food, punch and eggnog. Christmas now doesn't seem the same without this event.

Only once that I can remember during the 31 years the Navy was here was there any serious trouble and that was in October 1973, when a mini riot took place involving black v. white sailors. Some white sailors objected to black sailors dating white Scottish girls, and things boiled over one evening, resulting in several serious injuries. Usually, the Shore Patrol in cooperation with the local police, kept things pretty well in hand, and I don't remember us having the problems with youth crime and drugs that we have today.

Judging by the number of local girls who married Americans, and by the number of local people who now have friends or family in the US who they visit regularly, most local people have very positive memories of the 31 years the Americans were with us. Although some would not like to admit it, Dunoon's economy has never recovered fully since their departure, despite various attempts to bring new industries and new jobs to the area. They are sorely missed. ◻

Through close contact with Americans Dunoon people became sensitised to all the major events in the USA. When President Kennedy was elected in 1961, it seemed as though a new era was here. He was young and handsome and his wife was a glamorous and elegant young woman. We shared the excitement of the American girls at school at his election. After all, whoever was in the White House, his actions would affect our lives.

It wasn't long before all the apprehensions we'd felt at the arrival of this base were fulfilled when the Cuba Crisis began to develop in October 1962. The Soviet Union, it was discovered, was determined to have weaponry outposts as well, on her allies' soil and was busy shipping the missiles to Cuba. President Kennedy sent a military blockade to prevent any further transportation and we knew this was serious. We watched every news broadcast as the situation escalated day by day. President Kennedy appeared on our TV sets to explain why he was standing firm on this, as Kruschev, Russia's President became more belligerent. This was the situation we had been primed to dread. I remember a deep fear taking hold and my school friends and I talked endlessly about our impending doom. There was no comfort from parents or teachers. Mr Blair, the history teacher, used black humour to deflate the tension, setting homework with the words 'and that's for tomorrow if we're not blown to smithereens.' It's surprising how we laughed and how it made us feel better. The adults were just as frightened that the next move Russia made in retaliation would be a strike at the Holy Loch base. The newspapers were full of dramatic headlines. There seemed to be nowhere to turn.

As the blockade steamed towards its confrontation, one morning the *Proteus* and the submarines slipped out of the Holy Loch to the sea. Marian Dawes (née Paton) remembers watching them sailing out of the Clyde, and says, 'The fear that I experienced at that time is very relevant today. We were at the Ardenslate school when this happened and could see the ship. It must have been purgatory for the families when all leave was cancelled and everyone in the area felt we were very close to destruction.'

The target had been removed, to our relief. I hoped someone had told the Russians. When Kruschev backed down from the edge, the world knew we'd almost reached the logical conclusion of the arms race that had been going on since the Atomic age had arrived. The relief was indescribable but I remember feeling angry at the politicians who were making the world such a fearful place for children.

The *Proteus* returned in five days and things settled down somewhat. After this, some felt reassured about being under the wing of a superpower and others felt like dupes in some horrifying game. We still worried about accidents and there were a few of those to come over the years.

It was in November 1963 that brought the momentous event of President Kennedy's assassination. Dunoon Grammar School was a vale of tears as the young Americans mourned their loss and Scottish classmates felt very affected by their grief. He had been

Jim Collins (left) at the Holy Loch pier building in 1963. Later that year he met Mary Cunningham at the Espresso Cafe in Cardwell Bay and they married and later moved to USA

(below) Jim Collins with Mary Cunningham on his 1959 G3 Matchless and friends in 1964

Permission: Jim Collins

Jim Collins came to Holy Loch as a young, single serviceman and was assigned to the Liberty boats. He runs the Thistle Group website in memory of those days in Scotland

From all the messages and emails that I have read from the servicemen that had duty in Scotland, they say it was the best duty station in the US Navy.

I grew up in Scotland. Well, I arrived in Scotland at the age of 21, with no plans for the next two years. The whole process started in December 1960 when I joined the US Navy Reserves. On 1st August 1962 I reported to US Navy Receiving Station, Brooklyn, NY for active duty. I had an opportunity to request what I would like for a type of ship and a duty location and the first choice I was given was the USS *Proteus* and the location was Scotland.

Arriving at the ship in Scotland at zero dark hundred, that would be about 02:00 am, I was assigned to the boat division, and the 50 foot rag top which was an open boat with a canvas cover, didn't do much to keep the rain off, and the poor coxswain was out in the open.

From the 50 footer I moved to the Officer Motor Boat. That was nice, as you only had to make a boat run to the pier when an officer requested.

In January 1963 the second sub tender arrived in the Holy Loch. The USS *Hunley* came to relieve the USS *Proteus*. This was good news as I thought I was going back to the States. Little did I know that the Navy had other plans. I was transferred to the USS *Hunley* in February 1963.

In the boat division on the Hunley I was assigned to a boat called the Box 'L'. This boat was a World War II harbour mine layer. It was 64 feet, and looked like a small tug boat. Working on the Box 'L' I found two more cities in Scotland – Gourock and Greenock, as the Box 'L' made the run to Cardwell Bay.

The one thing that I miss when I go back to Scotland is the smell of the coal fires burning on a damp night. And one of the things I always look forward to is a fish supper – that is always the first meal I have when I return to Greenock.

Our liberty boat headed to Cardwell Bay one Tuesday night in May 1963 with another boat coxswain named Hank. He was talking about meeting Christine at the Espresso Cafe, and asked if I wanted to go with him. I said of course. The cafe had the best chocolate I have ever had.

When we got there I met Christine and her friend Mary and we all talked for some time. The following Friday night, again I met Mary at the Palladium Dance Hall, we had a good time and said I would meet her on Sunday May 12th.

When we met on Sunday Hank and Christine were there too. The day was warm and sunny, just a perfect day for a walk. So we started to walk, and walk we did all the way to Ashton and back. That was the start of the relationship between Mary and I. We were engaged on 28 Nov 1963, were married on 16 May 1964, and we now live in Connecticut on the beach.

Thistle Group website: www.Thistlegroup.net

inspiring for their generation with the start of the Peace Corps and his tackling of segregation. The younger teachers were sensitive and encouraged talking about this tragedy. We, again, felt connected to the American community and took the loss in a personal way with them. I remember collecting all the newspaper cuttings of the time. We wondered about a new President and his effect on our future.

When the USS *Proteus* was replaced by the USS *Hunley*, it was reported that her sailors had left enough unpaid bills to upset the Local Traders' Association. They said they were 'angry and disillusioned' and wouldn't be extending credit any more. Captain DuBois, Commanding Officer, had to respond and said these reports were exaggerated. 'There was a special effort before our departure to see that personnel paid any outstanding bills,' he said at a press conference, and offered to settle any overlooked payments.

A Carolina newspaper, *The News and Courier,* ran an article welcoming the *Proteus* home: 'Well done, *Proteus*' and stated, 'Not only were the officers and men of the *Proteus* called on to maintain the most exacting technical equipment, but they were subject to heavy pressures of an unusual kind. The *Proteus* became the target of spurious 'peace' groups in Great Britain that seek to disarm the Western Alliance. The crew of the *Proteus* behaved with dignity and restraint in the face of provocation.'

The USS *Hunley* arrived in 1963 and 250 *Proteus* servicemen wanted to stay on for another tour of duty. The submarine, the *Robert E Lee,* was leaving on a two

month patrol and signalled 'Welcome to the Southern lady.' The *Hunley* displayed a banner saying 'Gold to blue, ready to relieve you'.

The previous December, it had become clear that the Base was staying for some time to come as Parliament had voted against terminating the agreement with the American Government. It emerged that Great Britain would acquire her own Polaris submarine in return – a deal that had brought in the support of a large majority in the House of Commons. Furthermore, the signs were that structures were being put in place to provide leisure and shopping facilities for personnel and their families. A YMCA building was approved by the Town Council in 1963, and already in 1962 the old Ardnadam hotel had been converted into a social centre and commissary and exchange. The Safety Valve held some bitter feelings, probably because this new ship's arrival seemed to represent the dashed hopes of those who wanted Dunoon back as she was before these 'usurpers'. 'Let's face it,' wrote a local resident:

The Proteus and now the Hunley is in the Holy Loch for pleasure and home comforts for crew members, whilst off duty. Not because it is in the best strategic position.

Dunoon as a holiday resort has suffered tremendously due to the presence of these Americans in the area. Unfortunately, some of the local people – far too many indeed – will not look to the town's future as a holiday resort, as they should be doing. Instead of which they tolerantly brush aside even where American Forces are situated, they despoil and corrupt everything they come in contact with.

Fortunately, to my mind the Americans will not always be with us but that is one reason that this town should live up to its motto 'Forward', instead of grabbing upon the 'dangling dollar' which is presently held under our noses, and so eagerly grasped.

This was too much for one American who replied:

If you call Dunoon 'Pleasures and Comforts' I shudder to think what you call luxuries. My idea of home comforts is not constantly messing about with expensive coal and trying to get warm with a fireplace too small in the first place.

The Scottish travel folders in the US don't clue us in on the fact that Scotland is behind the times in many ways.

If Dunoon had any decent entertainment, such as a bowling alley or an indoor swimming pool, sailors as well as locals wouldn't be visiting the Court so often.

Can you expect us not to complain when your roads are full of holes and ruin tyres and shocks in a car. Your hamburgers taste like sawdust, and a cup of coffee – well, I'd rather not waste my money. Some local merchants and shopkeepers depend on our trade. It

seems you who are profiting are complaining.

As far as Americans taking advantage of your so-called domestic comforts, over 100 Scottish women married Proteus sailors and who knows how many will marry Hunley sailors. They don't appear to be broken up at the idea of leaving their homeland. Why should locals look to tourists for trade when they get it all year round from us?'

This in turn provoked another acerbic letter from a Dunoonite:

Re last week's letter from an American, I suppose when the writer came to the Holy Loch he or she thought we people were barbarians with heather sprouting out of our ears and only thistles as beds. What a rude awakening they got. Let the Americans remember, we have what they can never have – honour and glory. Let America remember 1942 when we stood alone and the mighty Americans profited.

I, as an ex-Proteus mother-in-law, could give quite a few facts regarding the cost of living in the USA. Suffice to say my daughter in her last letter wrote 'Don't let any Yank fool you. Their Almighty Dollar is nothing here.'

As a wife who lost her husband at Dunkirk, I feel much at the arrogance of many of the Americans. The truth is they have never had it so good and with commissions, duty free

Instead of Dunoon being Americanised,
Americans were being absorbed
into the Scottish ways of life

cigarettes and drink etc have no right to moan. Neither the district nor the people profit from having the American Navy here.

Mrs Margaret Robertson, in one of her many campaigning letters to the *Standard*, responded to a national politician's statement thus, in March 1963:

Lord Home's assertion that 'The Polaris submarine is our best assurance against war' is a very questionable statement.

How many nations are going to adopt this 'insurance policy' by acquiring nuclear weapons and then will Lord Home 'insure' us against involvement in nuclear incidents or accidents among these other nations?

Lord Home's assessment of the Polaris submarine, in fact, means that it is the most deadly threat to Russia that the west, so far possesses. Surely we have known this since it was introduced two years ago. At that time tension was appreciably easing between Russia and the West; but the military and armament clique in America, having developed their super-killer were not going to let a little matter of better relations between nations baulk them of their triumph, so the 'ultimate weapon' (with its resulting acceleration of the Arms race) was launched upon an already nerve-wracked world.

Meanwhile, in America, it was being reported in the pages of the *Christian Herald* that 'The US Navy

conquers Holy Loch'. Aboard the *Proteus,* the article went on, Captain Schlech, Commander of Submarine Squadron 14 based at Holy loch, was holding one of his regular receptions for members of the Town Council and notables of Dunoon. After lunch, the Scots would spend the afternoon with the officers and crew, discussing in an atmosphere of good will, any problems. 'Though the presence of the US Navy is amiably accepted today,' the article goes on, 'it was not always so.' But that was all part of the embarrassing past it implied and instead of Dunoon being Americanised, the opposite had happened and Americans were being absorbed into the Scottish ways of life. Their children were looking healthier with walking everywhere in the Scots weather.

The article went on to describe how the Navy won over the Scottish people, with a 'hundred small spontaneous acts'. For instance the crew of the *Los Alamos* were involved in raising money for Kirn Children's Home and one little girl in particular, who now had a trust fund. They gave shipboard parties for the kids. They did good works for elderly people . 'At every level, mutual affection runs deep.'

Whilst the sheer patronising tone of such reporting, and the false picture it may have given of the population being won over set people's teeth on edge, there was no doubt that human relationships were taking precedence over prejudice. Where person met person, sincere friendship and warmth were established irresistibly, and there were many good envoys.

Against the less desired correlations of living beside a foreign military base, the people it brought there often enriched local lives. The American Wives Club started an annual Art and Craft Show. The Holy Loch Singers were established. Individual Americans devoted their efforts to raising money for local charities and sport brought many young people together over the years. Some Americans even represented Scotland in school sports and Mark Mallory, a sailor, boxed for Scotland in 1980 and won the Scottish National Light Middleweight championship in 1981. A Marine, Leigh Gibson ran in the Glasgow marathon in 1983, and raised a big sum for a local charity. And in the small deeds and intricacies of daily life, many showed a neighbourliness and kindness unrecorded but not forgotten.

Art Bivens had taken command of the USS *Sam Houston* submarine in 1967. He describes how the American navy co-ordinated operations with the Royal Navy, who were based at the Gare Loch.

A four day sea trial and refresher training operation occurred near the end of a 28 day refit. The Holy Loch squadron of SSBNs conducted these operations mainly in the Firth of Clyde and the Irish Sea. The operational areas for US submarines were assigned by the Royal Navy. We got along well with our RN friends and occasionally visited one another. However, there were a few incidents which tested that friendship. One spring morning, my ship, *Sam Houston* and a British O-Class diesel-powered submarine got too close for comfort. We were returning to the Holy Loch from a four day sea trial and conforming to the buoyed channel in the Firth of Clyde. The British sub was headed out. Being a smaller ship with less draft, she decided to take a short cut through shallow water, but by doing so she cut across the channel and directly into our path. When I saw that she was not going to conform to the channel for a normal port to port passage I told the Officer of the Deck to stop engines and back down. Stopping 6500 tons isn't done quickly. 'Back Emergency' was ordered, but when it appeared that we might ram the other sub, I grabbed the microphone to the Engine Room and shouted 'Pour it on Manoeuvring!' With the reactor and main engines cranked up to 100% power the ship was shaking and creating a tremendous reverse wash. At the same time we were feverishly sounding the international emergency signal on our whistle. We didn't hit the British sub, but not by more than a few feet. Our bow was pointed directly at her mid-ship, when both of us had stopped. There wasn't a peep out of her, not a word, not a signal. She just took off and continued on her merry way. I have great respect for the British Navy but this near accident gave me an awful fright. As an ancient Greek philosopher said, 'a collision can ruin your whole day.'

Kate Wren and Bill Holloway in 1987.

The presence of so many US citizens brought out some of American society's strifes. Racism sometimes raised its ugly head. Desegregation in the US was only in its infancy in the early sixties and Dunoon was astonished at Americans' accepted rules. Christine MacCallum (née Kerr) remembers as a youngster, hearing a black sailor asking which side he should sit on in Juno's cafe. She says, 'That was when I first realised about colour segregation – having lead a sheltered life in Dunoon, I had just never come across it.'

In the late sixties, in parallel with the Civil Rights movement in the States, the young generation of black sailors wore their new consciousness unapologetically, challenging the unacknowledged but insidious racism that seemed to be still within the American military. There was more of them in the contingent by now and they socialised easily with local girls. This was intolerable to some white southern-born sailors.

I witnessed the resulting tensions personally when, as a young woman I entered the portals of that 'den of iniquity' known as the Enlisted Men's Club, at Ardnadam with a group of servicemen and their girlfriends. We went to hear some live music but I could feel an atmosphere of simmering tension between the group I was with and a group of black sailors sitting across the room. When I politely accepted an invitation to dance with a black sailor, the atmosphere worsened. It was obvious that I was being used as a provocation and neither side was behaving with distinction. This deeply ingrained strand in American life was being ripped out and the process

was going to be violent. What was more ominous was the perceived threat to the discipline onboard the ship where so much weaponry lay. These fears were exacerbated by a fire on the USS *Canopus* in 1970 that got so out of control that three people died including two black men, locked in the Brig. This contributed to the racial tension and appalled Cowal residents, especially when they found out that it happened next to stored missiles. Any reassurances were heard with great cynicism.

All this was a portent of things to come three years later, when in October 1973 the situation escalated and all the ingredients came together one Saturday night for a destructive confrontation and riot, between black and white sailors and local men, too. Dunoon's Argyll Street was the scene of running fights and the smashing of every window. A local man, uninvolved, was attacked and hurt. The numbers involved were small (around ten) but in a small town it made a horrible and incongruous impact. It was international news and Navy 'Bigwigs' were drafted in to mend this public relations disaster. The Commander of the Squadron wrote to the Provost of the day (John Dickson) with an abject apology. 'On behalf of the American government,' he wrote, 'I sincerely apologise for the disgusting conduct of a few American men last Saturday evening' and the Secretary of the Navy, no less, appeared in Dunoon to show how seriously he took this matter. The culprits appeared in the Sheriff Court, but in private.

The Vietnam War was also close to home for Dunoon people. People serving there were known. It wasn't the far away conflict that it might have been if we didn't have personal friends affected by it. My future father-in-law volunteered for duty in Vietnam and his daughter Betsy, who had been finishing her education in Dunoon, had to go home immediately.

In the 1960s as the western world's values and morals were challenged and revolutionised, so the distinctions between our society and American society became more blurred. Travel, technology but most of all music, were shortening the cultural distances between us and young people shared more with each other than with older generations. Any prejudiced stigma attached to dating sailors had diminished as more and more families welcomed American sons-in-law into their fold. Also as old fashioned strictures on accepted morality faded, there seemed less of a divide between the single sailors behaviour and society's in general.

As the seventies wore on, the police were paying less attention to matters of 'immoral houses' and more to the drug problem, now being solidly concentrated in the West of Scotland, emanating from the dealers finding lucrative sales around the Base haunts. The MOD police developed instincts and techniques for targeting any sailors carrying drugs aboard the ship.

One officer became known as the 'terrier' because he was relentless at sniffing out the guilty smugglers. On one occasion a sailor hadn't even climbed from his taxi when this officer stepped forward and pulled down his lower lip. Out fell some cannabis. He had an unerring radar and treated officers, sailors and visitors with the same suspicion. There was a hierarchy of security clearance status on board and serious punishment for offenders when caught. But the feelings of anxiety grew with the evidence.

Art Bivens (Captain, USN, Ret.) writes:

> The American people would have little confidence in its nuclear deterrents to war if they were believed to have officers or crewmen aboard who used illegal drugs. There would be concern that some crazy mavericks high on something would try to fire nuclear weapons. Even though there were plenty of safeguards to prevent an unauthorised launch there is, in addition the Personal Reliability Program. Medical and psychological evaluations of personnel both in their past and present, including no known use of illegal drugs, are in the program. There was zero tolerance for the use of drugs in the submarine force.

By 1974 the employees of McAlpine's had arrived to work at Ardyne, near Toward, on the construction of oil platforms, and some were causing havoc with their drinking, taking all the attention away from the servicemen. This was a secondary invasion and many comparisons were made, from which the Americans emerged – much to their amusement – as a preferable presence. The hard working, hard drinking 'navvies' played hard too and travelling on the Clyde ferries at that time could be an unpleasant experience, trapped on board with drunken louts for the twenty minute ride. They were the talk of the town with their shocking behaviour and the 'camp followers', who moved into Dunoon, out to part them from their money. It was not an added attraction for holidaymakers, and the town felt under siege and beleaguered. But it provided lucrative employment for locals and there was a lot more money being spent in the town.

The Base facilities were well established and American housing was being custom built for servicemen and their families through the 1970s. This took money away from the local economy in that rental accommodation wasn't at a premium any more, but there was still a need for hotel accommodation and officers' housing. There was a large fleet of taxis operating in the town, as locals had got lazy too and now thought nothing of using them every day. Late night food, such as fish and chip shops and restaurants prospered. There was no doubt either that local shops catering for American tourists, here to see family, gained business. There is even a Polaris tartan.

However, although it suited the American authorities to project the perception that thousands of dollars were being pumped into the local economy, some argued that this was a myth. The Americans were self-sufficient in food and alcohol and bowling alleys and now housing, they said, so why couldn't they pay for their own school and medical facilities, particularly for all the births occurring. It was straining our resources and any rise in the rates was blamed on these causes, even though the authorities denied it.

It didn't help that local people were not allowed to share in the American facilities. As GG Giarchi states in his book *Between McAlpine and Polaris*, 'Demands upon public and community services escalated because the American families had a disproportionate share of local services.' This was really a failing of governments to address these issues as individual servicemen could not be denied education for their children or maternity services for their wives.

The Poseidon missile system replaced the Polaris one in the seventies and new anxieties were raised. It was described as a big advance in weaponry, and the secretary of the US Navy visited the base in 1974 for an inspection tour. Nothing had changed with a Labour government, despite the fact that in the early days many of the CND campaigners were Labour politicians. So as time went on it was becoming more a part of the landscape. In fact a selection of postcards were now on sale showing the Base as a tourist attraction, and for some it was.

In the 1980s female personnel came on board, including Commanders. Commander (Dr) Laurel B Clark, who later died in the *Columbia* mission disaster in 2003, was stationed in Holy Loch. During her Holy Loch assignment, she dove with US Navy divers and Naval Special Warfare Unit Two Seals and performed numerous medical evacuations from submarines. She is remembered with great warmth by the people who knew her, and seemed to love Scotland.

Throughout the years of the Base, American Intelligence Services had a foothold in the Dunoon area to protect the Base from Russian spies. In 1963, it was reported in the local paper that Captain Syverson of the USS *Hunley* had ordered that two hotels in Dunoon, the Argyll and the Queen's, were out of bounds to servicemen on security grounds, for the duration of an STUC conference. This was because four Russian Trade Unionists were staying there. This may seem a paranoid reaction now but this was indicative of the atmosphere at the time.

Anyone who might anxiously inquire about the dangers of radiation leaks and what was being dumped in the Loch could come under their scrutiny or that of our own Special Branch.(It emerged in recent years that Special Branch had all of CND's plans of campaign against the Base's arrival.)

No-one was inclined to believe the Ministry of Defence and the American Navy's reassurances about there being no pollution. There was a feeling of 'well, they would say that, wouldn't they?' No government wants to alarm the population, and I do not remember ever being instructed about mass evacuation in the worst possible scenario of a radiation accident. Human beings going about their daily lives push fears of a silent, invisible killer sweeping across the area out of their minds, or move away. Or commit to campaign against it with all the consequences that might bring to their lives, if it is considered to be against the interests of the State.

Of course some believe that any risks are all part of modern life and that things cannot be un-invented, that it all has to be weighed against the benefits of a balance of power. Both outlooks can be found in Cowal and surprisingly, in retired servicemen.

In the years since the Base left in 1992, the MOD instigated a three year clean-up operation of Holy Loch, as a great deal of objects large and small went overboard, accidentally or as rubbish. It has been controversial as some experts believed that if contaminated material lay there it may be best to leave well alone. As the MOD has always denied that there was any, it maintains that all the debris has been removed. But not everyone is convinced of this and surmise that perhaps it has been decided to allow anything sinister to stay buried in the deep waters, so that we are living with an unknown legacy.

When the Cold War began to thaw, the Iron Curtain came down, and weaponry systems changed, it was clear that the Base would be wound up. But it still came as a shock. The *Dunoon Observer* headline read 'Base Bombshell' in 1991. It was strangely ironic that the same headline could have applied thirty years before when the Base was proposed, but now the fears concerned its departure. It called for action to help the area survive this enormous adjustment, with estimated civilian job losses of 800 in total, and £11 million a year input. An inevitable dependency had grown but the US government took no responsibility, stating that Federal law forbade compensating other countries for Base closures.

The American Navy went to great lengths to withdraw from the community graciously. A departure ceremony was arranged for 21st February 1992, attended by Admiral JM Boorda, Commander in Chief of US Naval Forces in Europe and Vice Admiral Sir Hugo White, flag officer Scotland and Northern Ireland, and many other dignitaries. Some officers who had been stationed in Holy Loch in the past, came back for the event. It marked the end of a 30-year relationship, love-hate in some ways, but rich in texture and tapestry.

One thousand families were leaving. The *Los Alamos* dry dock was transported out across the Atlantic in February and the USS *Simon Lake* departed in March 1992. We drove by to see the 'empty' Loch.

A warm tribute appeared in the *Dunoon Observer* from a local resident, to the US wives. They had played a very important part, she said.

> Whilst the husbands did their jobs, you the wives were left to get on with it. It, being the making of a house, a home and the problems of adapting to a different way of life for you and your children when you were so far from family and friends. Despite all that you gave freely of your time to care for people in the community, in particular children, the elderly and disabled. I recall all your hard work and imaginative ideas in fund raising, successfully culminating in your generous donations to the various local charities. Ladies, grateful thanks to you for all your kindness and generous hospitality. We have happy memories of your stay here in Scotland.

There were decisions to be made about all the buildings and houses and how to tackle the future. Many business people had strong ideas about the way forward and it was hard to find a consensus sometimes.

Now that Cowal has come through those difficult times a perspective is developing about the 30 years of the base and now that it is history it can be unravelled, analysed and considered.

Petty officer David Bernett contemplates life away from Scotland as the support ship USS *Simon Lake* prepares for the US Navy's pull-out from the Holy Loch in 1992

Tom Reid was a schoolboy when the base arrived. His whole social life changed when he made American friends as did his parents

My first memory of the American invasion was the day the *Proteus* sailed into the Holy Loch. I was about 12 or 13 and we had been given the day off school to view the ship coming in. We were very excited and had great expectations. I remember being on my bike with other school friends at Ardnadam Point and watching this monstrosity come into the Loch. It was so ugly. We expected a sleek battleship with funnels and huge guns and instead we had a box-like thing.

Shortly after its arrival there was a town meeting at the Burgh Hall given by the US Navy to explain what was in the loch and introduce themselves. Many of us trudged along and filled the hall. There were refreshments *a la* US military – free pop and sodas and doughnuts and all kinds of sweet things we had never seen before. The officers showed us a Polaris missile and explained how we were perfectly safe as they could not explode on their own. Sigh of relief . . . more coke and doughnuts. They promised we would all get along and that the families would start arriving in a few months, so be nice to the boys in town.

My birthday is 3rd July and I will always remember my first 4th. The US had been in town almost a year and were having a big 4th of July celebration out by Innellan and the whole town was invited. I'd be about 13 and a couple of friends and I decided to go along. We were walking along the shore road on our way to Innellan when a huge big Yankee car pulled up. Chauffeur-driven with a big old guy in the backseat. Said he was some mucky-muck with the navy and did we want to go to a picnic? We never let on we were on our way so he gave us three wee ragamuffins a lift in his huge Yankee car.

There was a huge barbecue set up with hot dogs, hamburgers and chicken all grilling away. Mountains of coke and barrels of ice, salad, desserts aplenty. We had never had a barbecue and a hamburger was just unknown. As for all the free coca cola we were in awe. A mountain of cases and cases of all kinds of pop. FREE! Unheard of. Who are these people? Must be rich!

We ate all we could then we filled bags with coke and pop and buns and anything else we thought we could carry and took off across the fields heading back home for Dunoon with more stories about these weird Americans and all the FREE stuff we took. Paying attention to hide in bushes when a car passed because we just knew this was too good to be true and they were looking for us and the stolen coca cola. When I got home I couldn't stop telling my folks about all the free food and drink and there was so much it was scary.

Then I learned there was more as you got older. And they did not begrudge you helping yourself and were only too happy to share their huge abundance of wealth, in my eyes at least. This was so against Scottish culture and capabilities at that time. Most Scots didn't have a fridge, or a telly or a car or a phone and here was a whole pile pouring into wee Dunoon who had all that and more. Big changes.

I remember that my folks rented to an enlisted sailor and his wife from Kentucky and we were so taken with them. We used to rent to holiday makers but that was all over now and we had no option but to rent to the Americans. That and the fact we could gouge them in rent because the navy was paying for it. The Kentuckians were like Martians to us. The wife had huge hair and we couldn't understand a word she said. He played the fiddle and eventually we had some good times together. . . right up until they painted our old Victorian furniture black enamel. Faither didn't approve of that and next we had a black Chief and his family move in. Big Smitty and his wife and two wee boys. My mother was over the moon. She was so glamourous and he was huge, plus the wee boys were darling. Mum glommed onto them because of their exoticness, that and the fact we had never seen a black person before. The black contingent all hung together. There wasn't many of them but they chose Mum's house as the meeting place and she was in heaven. Boy, could they dress and have a good time. First time I ever saw a guy in a green suit. . .Wow! Mum went to a baby shower once, the only white gal, and came back with a blue cake. We didn't eat it! Mum felt obliged to take it when offered, but we wouldn't eat it. Strange people who eat blue cake and have jelly with vegetables for a salad. I mean, come on.

I made many friends with the American kids. We had moved to the new Grammar School and there was ten times the amount of kids. They all seemed so much more mature than us and certainly were more worldly. I balanced my friendships as evenly as possible with Scottish and American kids but slowly a rift appeared where the Scots started to ask for either one or the other as friends. I couldn't care what they thought and became more entrenched with the Yanks who were much more fun and more interesting. Their parents organised a club for us to hang out at over what is now the Observer's shop on John Street and Argyll Street. I think it was called something like Psi Sigma Chi (never did ask what that meant). But we were card-carrying and could go upstairs to the club and hang out. I believe they had a pool table and library and music. As a member of this club we were entitled to attend dances which were held at first in a Quonset hut across from the fire station. These were fun and we danced to the latest UK and US hits. Much of the US hits had not been heard over in Scotland before – the Righteous Brothers, Beachboys, Sandra Dee, Chubby Checker and more. All the 60s hits. We put on acts and lip-synced the bands.

The folks running the club were the nicest and most caring parents I had ever met, and they were so naive to the goings on they were sitting ducks. They organised a bus trip up to Glasgow to see the Rolling Stones. They wouldn't let us go see the Beatles because they thought that would be dangerous, and maybe wrong, so they allowed us to see the Rolling

The American Years

Stones. Bless them! What a scene! There was about 15 of us and we were in line and they are almost all Yanks. These Glaswegian boys just flipped over the girls and the awffy nice chaperones were wishing they had brought a gun. Into the old Alhambra I think it was, with its plush seats and the screaming is insane! The noise is overwhelming and the poor chaperones are trying to make some kind of order out of all this and it isn't working. It was fantastic.

Never before could I have gone to a Rolling Stones concert in Glasgow because the stupid ferry system stopped at 8 pm. Being with the American club we took a US Navy launch back to Dunoon at around midnight. I couldn't sleep that night for thinking of where I had been. Kids from Dunoon did not get to go see the Rolling Stones in Glasgow on a Saturday night! This was magic! On Sunday I got up and did my paper round at 7 am and was smiling from ear to ear. I had seen something that none of my Dunoon peers had ever seen and it has stayed with me all these years.

The club and I went a second time months later to another rock show but the first one stayed with me. If it had not been for the American club, Psi Sigma Chi. . . and its fear of the Beatles, I would never have realised my (don't want to say difference) individuality? drive? eccentricity? originality? guts? to be even willing to take on the outside world. These gracious people helped me so much in building my self esteem and when it came time for me to say to Canada . . . yeah sure I'll emigrate. . . my main thought was, I will be close to America.

The cars! God were they magnificent. Sooooooo big! And beautiful. We, as you know, have narrow streets, and these huge T Birds and Chevies and Oldsmobiles were not built for our roads. The Messersmiths were way cool and had a Peugot car. Mrs Messersmith would pick me up around Cammesreinach Brae on the way to school so I timed it where she would meet me much sooner at the top of Hamilton Street and I could cut off a good cold half mile walk.

I met the Cushman girls! Their father was Executive Commander of the *Hunley*, second ship in the Holy Loch. He had an apartment for a cabin on board ship and was the nicest guy. I called him Uncle Chuck behind his back, and he found out about it and just laughed. He asked me once if I would ever think about enlisting in the US Navy, I could become a US citizen in two years and the navy would be good for me. I said fine to that if. . . I could be stationed in Dunoon those years and he was my commander. Again he just laughed. So I didn't join. Because of his rank on board and my friendship with his daughters I was invited on board ship one Sunday for brunch. I got all dressed up and met the girls and their mother at Ardnadam Pier where we were picked up by his launch to take us on board. We were whistled on board and led to his cabin. It was fabulous, with a bedroom and and office and living room and toilet, shower and all furnished that American way with clean lines and subdued colours with little table lamps and bowls of fruit and candy, plus the requisite fridge bursting with coca cola. . . anything we wanted. We were then led to the Captain's table where about 12 people were sitting. I was the only Scot. Linen napkins and little coloured waiters who jumped if you raised an eyebrow. I had my first grape juice that morning and was hooked. I was a bit of a freak show for the officers wearing my Carnaby Street suit and big wide tie but they were very gracious. These little Filipino guys, just kept on bringing food and the Captain said to me I could have anything I wanted and to bring me more grape juice. What a life, I thought. So as I relaxed more I said to the Captain, 'How come all these little waiters look alike and there aren't any white guys?' Pleasantly enough I thought. . . just asking. Big hush over the table and the Captain says. . . 'because they are good at it – let's go watch a movie!' So off we trot down a few flights of stairs, below deck, to a cinema with seating for about 40. A cinema! Jeez! I was blown away. I had never even thought of a cinema and we watched – I forget what movie now – but it was a year before it came to Dunoon. We were served popcorn and sweeties and fruit and the ever popular Coca Cola. Do you maybe think coke is owned by the military, or vice versa?

When we left we were again picked up by the Captain's launch and ferried back to Sandbank and driven home. Wow! I was hooked. I was invited many times back on board and was always treated kindly. Eventually I was able to move about the ship on my own and would run up deck to the Commander's cabin for candy or pop while we watched the movies. I was never asked what I was doing or who I was as I ran up those stairs and crossed decks in my civvies and

only once did I run down one too many stairs and was faced with two nervous armed sailors with rifles and a NO Admittance sign at a door standing guard. I quickly excused myself and ran back upstairs but remember their astonished looks as I appeared and disappeared. No-one chased me or ordered me to stop. Here I am on board a Polaris missile ship in a blue double-breasted Carnaby Street suit and long hair and nothing happens! Changed days.

I spent many happy and continually amazed years with the Americans, invited to their homes, parties and lives in Dunoon. It's strange but I only remember their being so courteous and kind, not to mention gracious and foreign. Some had lived in Honolulu. The mere idea of Honolulu or Norfolk, Virginia, or anywhere else in the world I had never been! These kids had travelled and I was IMPRESSED. Remember Dunoon had lived in isolation for a century. Holiday makers came in the summer and we had Dunoon to ourselves for the rest of the year. Not so with the Americans. They were here all year long. Year in and out. Eventually we as a town started to lose our identity and name and were given another one we didn't approve of or deserve. Things change. . . . The turn around came when the *Simon Lake* brought over a different sort of crew with less families. I was also ready to leave Dunoon myself and the years after the *Hunley* left were only grabbed from visits home. But I never changed my idea of the Americans. I had been groomed by the finest the US Navy had sent over.

The American Years

Doug Ebert, Past President, Site One Holy Loch Scotland Association

"the sense of belonging, security, and the warm feeling of being a part of it all made it a great place to live"

I arrived in Scotland for the first time in Oct. '83, I had tried for nearly eighteen years to get assigned to the Holy Loch. In my final tour before retirement my detailer finally said I could go. So with my retirement cancelled I took orders to the *Hunley* AS-31 and went to Scotland.

On first arriving I was taken by how everything seemed like the movies – the old buildings, the countryside right into town. I was a bit put out at first as it took some time to get settled and find a place to live. I was informed there was a place for me in Sandbank, right near the ship! I could walk to work everyday, great!

Life was lived in a gentle easy pace and I adapted well to it and could not wait to get away from the ship and on the 'beach'. I came to know many people and made many friends while on my first tour in Scotland and still have them after all these years.

I think the most that impressed me my first time there was the honesty of the people and trust. Now I am not talking about up in Glasgow and Govan, but in the countryside and wee towns. I could go along on a Saturday and visit the shops, collect my messages and leave them in my motor with the windows down and they would be there when I was ready to leave town. I never locked my door the 2+ years I was there the first time!

I have one experience that impressed me the most. I was over in Tighnabruaich and I saw an item in a shop that I really wanted but did not have enough money with me. I asked the shopkeeper if he would hold it for me if I left a deposit. He said, 'Here, take it and when you get the money, come back and pay me!'

I could not believe it. He did not know me from Adam and I was from the other side of the mountain, yet he told me to take it. Well I did and I went straight home and got the money and drove right back. When I arrived, he was surprised and when I paid him he said, 'I didna mean for you to come right back, I trust you.' Well I was impressed and have been ever since.

In 1985 I was under orders to leave and in 1990 I finally made it back via Sardinia and this time I found a place to live over in Strachur on the estate of Sir Fitzroy McLean and I just loved it out there in the village. I did not want to leave and I even looked at property over in Kilfinan to buy and make into a B&B but affairs of the heart took over and the base closed. I left with a heavy heart for I really did want to retire there and spend the rest of my life and I would today if I could convince my wife whom I met there to move back.

Again the sense of belonging, security, and the warm feeling of being a part of it all made it a great place to live. I was involved with the activities in the village and with the Fete that was held on the estate every Spring and I just loved it. The hills up behind the village were a lovely place to walk and view the beautiful Loch Fyne and across to Inveraray. I just always felt secure and as if I was home.

After we left the loch for the last time I went on and retired but could not get the longing for returning out of me. So after five years I decided to see if there were others such as myself that would like to go back for a reunion. A lot of them did and in 2001 we held our first reunion in Dunoon and we are going to have another in 2005!

George Johnstone was a teenager in 1961. He married Betsy, the daughter of the Master Diver on the *Hunley*, and they have lived in London for many years

My earliest recollection relating to the arrival of the US Polaris base in Holy Loch was not the sight of a large grey ship sailing up the Clyde but of anti-bomb protesters arriving in our small town. Many had the appearance of students or beatniks and they marched along the Shore Road to sit in relatively silent protest at the foot of Ardnadam Pier. It was not a large gathering but the numbers were swollen by the attendance of police and the press. I remember the subsequent photographs appearing in the newspapers included one or two of my schoolmates, and in particular my classmate Brian Wilson.

Within days, clusters of Navy personnel started to appear in our midst conveyed to our town centre by a cavalcade of taxis that had mystically materialised overnight. The sailors' uniforms mirrored those that I had seen on the cinema screen as did both the accents and behaviour of the servicemen. Smoking a Pall Mall, lit by the fashionable Zippo lighter became *de rigueur* in local bars and cafes.

Hotel bars that had previously proved unpopular with local townsfolk became regular venues for sailors on 'shore leave' where they met young ladies who had come across from the Scottish mainland by ferry in search of more interesting leisure activity than was available in their home towns.

Several weeks after the arrival of the depot ship, the first children of the officers and senior enlisted men arrived in our school. Apparently when the US Navy set about establishing a new base overseas, officers and crew were closely vetted to minimise the likelihood of civil disturbance. That seemed very much the case to me with all of the early Americans (both grown ups and children) proving ultra friendly almost as if they had been trained to win over the support of the local residents.

Apart from the token Ban the Bomb protests I can't recollect sensing a feeling of resistance to the arrival of the American base from the local townsfolk. Informed comment suggested that the Holy Loch had been chosen not only for its strategic advantage in offering missile range across Europe and relatively quick access to the Baltic zone but also because the Cowal Peninsula was showing signs of economic decline from the downturn in tourism as more Scottish families chose to holiday abroad.

My particular recollections include:

Fashion – buttoned-down collars, white socks and loafer shoes, crew cuts for the boys and curled hair for the girls, 'Bobby' socks with high heels and sweat shirts.

Basketball was added to the school sports curriculum.

4th of July celebrations financed by US Navy with sporting equipment freely provided in the form of softball bats and gloves and American footballs, free hotdogs and Budweiser beer.

The local economy was boosted by the dollar, escalating the price of rented accommodation which in turn provided for the improvement of local housing including the introduction of window insulation and oil heaters to make the room temperature more amenable.

The creation of the Commissary changed the cultural taste of the local population (hot dogs, iced tea, mayonnaise, dill pickles, Hersheys canned chocolate, peanut butter and marshmallows).

Topics of discussion served to widen understanding of other religions (eg Mormons, Quakers) and different cultural outlooks and ways of living from around the world.

Slam books which served to identify the 'in crowd' from the 'also rans', added to the conceit of the popular and the despair of the insecure but nonetheless held greater attraction than Maths or French.

The 'Y' club, or the Psi Sigma Chi club, which was the forerunner of youth clubs in the community and provided recreational activity for the American kids and their Scottish friends (by invitation only).

A new vocabulary, which included such descriptive words as 'restriction 'and 'slumber party'.

A west coast Californian liberation and sexual promiscuity which was alien to my Scottish Presbyterian upbringing but which peer pressure forced me to endure!

George Johnstone and Betsy Messersmith

Betsy Johnstone (née Messersmith) came to Dunoon as a schoolgirl, when her father was stationed at Holy Loch

I lived in Dunoon with my family from December 1962 until August 1965 (aged 14 to 17) and then returned by myself in August 1966 until March 1967 (aged 18) when I had to go back to the States because my father was going to Vietnam.

This story has to be set in context. The background of the Americans that came to Dunoon in the 1960s has always been left out. This is a strange thing because people in Dunoon set each other in generational family context all the time.

Our family and every other Navy family, unless it was their first posting, had lived many places and without extended family support. Many had lived in Guam, Japan, Hawaii as well as the continental US. My family had lived in Hawaii twice which only matters in the sense that we had lived in a very different environment. The other strange thing was we never talked about these places, even amongst other Americans. Those places were gone and we were in Scotland. In the year before my family reached Dunoon we had lived in Iowa, Maryland and Virginia. I went to a German Lutheran School in Iowa for three weeks.

Arriving in Scotland late in December 1962 was a culture shock. We had flown to Prestwick on a military propeller airplane and it was a very long and noisy flight. A minibus met us and drove us to Dunoon. The driver used quaint terms, for instance a church we passed was 'modern of design'.

The flat Mrs Riley was renting to us, the upstairs of Mars Hill, had one coal fire but she was very welcoming. It had been a small hotel and Blanche Riley knew how to look after people. A great many sausage rolls made their way up the common staircase, not to mention Christmas cake. This overwhelmed my mother who was not used to being looked after. She was a Navy wife and always away from her parents.

We joined Blanche and Will Riley for New Year's Eve, with their young friends, Marion and Dugie, who had just announced their engagement. We watched a play on the tellie called 'Johnnie jibed the giblet' with the man who played Dr Finlay. (I couldn't understand a word of it and found that very worrying. I had been quite good at pidgin English in Hawaii.)

Of course the winter of 1962-63 is still known as a very cold winter and we had time off school because of snow. The old Grammar School looked like a castle to me and the rooms, a maze. The classroom with the hole in the wall you passed messages through was like something in a film. Mr Smith, the Headteacher, put me in 2C1, my mother having refused to let him put me back to 1st year.

I was to do French and as they were in their second year of French I had a tutor at home until the next year when I joined the class. I knew about decimals but failed Arithmetic as pounds, shillings and pence certainly made no sense at all. I received no help with this but the next term I doubled my mark. I probably remember this because I was embarrassed to fail.

Teachers were very nice to me. Geography was interesting and luckily we were studying America (it struck me that we had never studied Great Britain in the States). I tried to correct the pronunciation like Me-a-me (Miami), Florida but the teacher would not accept my advice.

At first my friends were mainly from Strachur and as they took people very much as they found them I wasn't treated as a stranger. My classmates in 2C1 remain in my memory very, very clearly which must mean it was a time of having to think about the situation. Of course I was a bit exotic, all the Americans were, as the *Proteus* had not been there long and the

The American Years

crew of the USS *Hunley* were arriving bit by bit.

There was a great deal of anti-Americanism in the town in general. Well, as a 14 year old I might have been sensitive. At that age you want to be like everyone else. I found that if I kept my mouth shut I was fine. I remember being sent to pick up some dry cleaning for my mother and the assistant and the customer already in the shop were having a very upsetting conversation, probably about the women who were coming to the town and the sailors. I racked my brain for the shortest utterance to get the clothes without being recognised as an American.

The women who came across to Dunoon were certainly amazing to me. The beehive hair, the fishnet stockings, the high heels and incredible winkle-pickers and the general obviousness of their business was shocking. My father had been in the Navy all of my life, perhaps we lived away from things, but I had never seen prostitutes before. I remember standing with my mother in the Loch Striven lodge which the Americans used for 4th of July picnics and these women standing near us talking loudly about their sailors. My mother and I were affronted.

American parents tried to keep a tight rein on their children as there were cultural differences in Dunoon. I don't think they were aware of the strong church youth clubs in the town. Going to Juno's Cafe which was the place to see and be seen was only allowed at certain times.

Americans tried to keep their children near home from the beginning. The large room that had been converted into a kitchen in our flat in Mars Hill was busy most nights with Scottish friends eating peanut butter sandwiches and pizza. A group of mainly Officers' daughters and Scottish boys formed and the boys spent time going from house to house.

I remember 22nd November, 1963 when Kennedy was shot as a typical American social occasion. Bonnie McConnell, my best American friend, was having a slumber party, girls staying overnight, you couldn't really say sleeping. Her parents were having a cocktail party in the sitting room. Because the parents were there boys were allowed to stay for a while. Suddenly the parents called us in and we watched what was happening on the television. I had idolised the Kennedys. To the Navy men there it must have seemed impossible that their Commander-in-Chief had been shot dead like that.

My Scottish girlfriends and I would mainly see each other in school. With separate girls' and boys' playground at the old school, break time would have to be with your girlfriends as talking across the fence to the boys was frowned upon. Rather we looked at them which was probably more interesting. I would also see girlfriends on Saturdays, in the town, or go to Glasgow, worried about wearing the wrong colour and upsetting Rangers or Celtic supporters.

My father was very keen that we would use the opportunity of living in Europe and we flew to Frankfurt on a military flight and rented a car. We visited Germany, Switzerland, Austria, Luxembourg,

France and Italy camping wherever we went. Probably Vienna was the highlight. We also toured in England, eg Plymouth, Northumbria, Stonehenge, St Michael's Mont and Stratford-upon-Avon.

The YMCA and Chaplin Beddingfield had a strong place in our lives. The YMCA was run by Mike Ellis who was a terrific influence on the young people who joined the club for teenagers. It was very much a mix of American and Scottish young people and Mike kept it interesting. We had philosophical discussions and social occasions. We played snooker on a small snooker table and table tennis, watched films, had dances including the quite formal Christmas Ball in 1963 at the Royal Marine Hotel, folk nights and we went to Glasgow on a coach to see the Searchers and Rolling Stones. The Gay Nineties Night featured a version of the can-can from Scottish and American girls and there was a 'casino'.

My mother helped Chaplain Beddingfield twice with his pastoral duties by looking after babies to give their young mothers' respite. These women had no extended family support unless their parents could afford to fly from America which did not happen often.

I went with an American girlfriend to Scottish Country dancing in the Burgh Hall. That was interesting. People were very helpful, as they are, pushing you gently to be in the correct place. I was very embarrassed when my feet went off the ground and I had to be landed when skirling round.

Politically I was a Scottish Nationalist, with 'End English Domination' stickers on my bedroom mirror and on the tops of my leather boots. Mrs Riley was upset about this as she had lived in Dunoon since the Second World War and was a great Royalist. She read the *Scottish Daily Express* and was very Tory in her views.

At school, Miss (then Mrs) MacDonald treated us like adults once she had worked out who was really interested. The other really important influence at school was Mr Blair. I had Archie for English, History and Modern Studies and he had a terrible time getting his pupils to discuss their views in class. Everyone would be sitting there not really sure what he wanted but I was always there for him, whether I knew what I was talking about or not. Please remember that I had read *The Enemy Within* by J Edgar Hoover when I was 12 and believed every word of the Communist threat. I particularly remember defending the bombing of Nagasaki and Hiroshima.

My parents loved Scotland and took hundreds of photographs of sunsets over the Clyde, the hills around Glencoe and North Uist in the nearly twenty years they lived in Dunoon, especially after dad retired from the Navy in 1975. I married into a local (although they only came to Dunoon 70 years ago) family 34 years ago and I have known them for nearly 40 years. I am still a Yank sometimes and that is strange for an American.

The American Years

"That is what I remember the most,
how the Americans were full of fun
and enjoyed life"

Ray Ahern (née Stewart) was a schoolgirl living beside the Holy Loch, in the village of Strone, when the *Proteus* arrived. She later married a serviceman and moved to the USA. She lives in Denver, Colorado

I remember going on the bus from Strone to Dunoon and the bus stopping at Ardnadam pier. All you could see was a sea of white hats bobbing up and down the full length of the pier, and the double decker bus was packed! At 11 years old I was awe-struck! Listening to the accents and smelling the strange (Winston) cigarettes that popped and cracked as they were smoked.

I met many, many, very nice American girls at school whose fathers were in the service. We loved the way they dressed and the loafers with the penny in the front of them. I befriended a girl called Rebecca Burnett, from Austin, Texas, and her ambition in life was to become a stripper! I lost touch with Becky when she left four years later, and I have always wondered if she accomplished her goal. When having dinner at her house it was the first time I had tasted the vegetable, corn! I loved it immediately. They were astonished that I had never tasted it before. Also the huge chocolate cakes her mother made from a 'cake-mix' box. Amazing! I also got to teach them how to build a coal fire – they were clueless! Their 'candy' was something I was not envious of, and I had the pleasure of introducing Cadbury's chocolate to Becky who became an instant addict. We used to look for

lemonade bottles to cash in and buy a small bar of Cadbury's chocolate.

The sound that bellowed from the Ardnadam Hotel as we passed on the bus sounded like so much fun. That is what I remember the most, how the Americans were full of fun and enjoyed life.

As it turned out, many years later I married an American myself and have lived happily in Colorado for over 30 years, going home to Scotland every chance I get. I have three wonderful sons who are very proud of their Scottish heritage.

When I first arrived in the States it was my first time overseas and when the door of the Pan-Am plane opened this rush of warm air hit me. I thought they had put a heater on at the door as I had never in my life felt warm air like that. I actually felt faint and the stewardess offered me a cup of water.

We drove in my husband's wee sports car that he had bought in Scotland and had shipped to Charleston, South Carolina, on our way to Cleveland, Ohio where his family were. We actually passed a chain gang in Virginia. I was spellbound as I gazed at the chains around those prisoners' wrists and ankles! Also, the tobacco leaves were hanging out to dry, stuff you would only see on documentaries at home!

Talk about culture shock when we arrived in Cleveland. On my first visit out to a Mall I could not take my eyes off the gun strapped to the policeman who was on patrol. I kept thinking, that is a REAL gun, I wonder if he has shot anyone. I was petrified!

My husband had to keep an eye on me in the grocery store as I had the tendency to put lemons and limes in the same bag to save using two bags! He would tell me that the store would think I was trying to steal one or the other. I tell you, I was a nervous wreck. I had never seen such a large selection of food under one roof. The refrigerators in the apartments seemed huge to me, also there was air-conditioning and garbage disposals. . . a whole new way of life!

We stayed in Ohio for a few years then moved to beautiful Colorado. The Rocky Mountains made me feel at home right away. I knew I could live here. When I go up in the mountains I feel that I am back home with all the trees and lakes around! My father used to call a blue sky at home a 'Colorado Sky' as he visited us a couple of times and was in awe of the blue, blue sky. He was also more than a little upset to find out that Scotch whisky was cheaper in the States than at home!

Americans are a very curious lot, and love to ask you where you are from when they hear you speak and are so eager to talk to you about your life here. I find myself doing the same thing when I hear a Scottish accent when I am shopping. My mum comes over to see me and to shop! She loves the shopping choices and the prices, and there is always a sale somewhere! She also commented on how polite the assistants in the shops were, compared to Scotland. Usually, she has to buy an extra case to take all her goodies home with her, and loves to say, Have a nice day! I still enjoy the American people and their way of life and often wonder how my life would have been without the American experience!

Margaret Davies (née Lyon) was a schoolgirl in 1961. She has lived in Canada since 1966

The one incident which is still very vivid in my mind is the day the ship sailed up the Clyde and a bunch of us from the Grammar School cycled to the Holy Loch and watched it sail past. I know we were wearing 'Ban the Bomb' badges and were not happy about having a Polaris Base so close to home. I remember it was quite a novelty to see the American sailors walk around town in their very distinct uniforms. It was 'just like the movies'.

When the American kids came to our school that was a novelty too. I remember that they were very friendly (a bit too friendly when they stole our boyfriends!) and introduced us to Slam Books! I also got into babysitting for the first time (as in watching children and actually getting paid for it!) for an American family across the road. They lived in the specially built flats for the Americans in William Street.

I treasure a very precious newspaper clipping that I have kept in my writing case since I left Dunoon all these years ago.

It shows the school trip to Switzerland and in the top picture it shows Eileen, Margaret, Christine, Jeanette and Maureen and in the bottom picture we see 'four young Americans'. That was a wonderful trip. Stevie Barrett was sharing my bedroom. The Americans also introduced us to penny loafers, saddle shoes and bobby sox, none of which we copied!

George B Walton, Jr. (Willie)

The only part of my arrival that I remember clearly was the late Commander Luther B. Sisson, Weapons Officer, ComSubRon 14, and his wife Helen (Bunny) meeting me with their huge nine seat Chevrolet Impala station wagon at Prestwick. In this particular case the first clear memory for me was Bunny (Well, Bunny to the adults, but since I was a 'damn teenager', her words, I was to call her Aunt Bunny, as I do gladly to this day) telling me in no uncertain terms to put out my. cigarette. 'George, I know your parents don't let you smoke!' I remember vividly my face turning redder than the tip of the offensive item.

I remember the house that was to be our home for the coming year. It was about halfway up the hill, with Hunter's Quay way down and off to the left when looking out the huge living room window. A gorgeous view. Boyd and I shared a bunk bed. Although not true, it seemed that the entire time I was living there that his atractive sisters lived way, way on the other side of the house. Sigh.

The YMCA is my next memory. I had been in Dunoon for only a few hours before I was taken up the stairs there. I was made to feel at home right away. Unbelievable! Everybody seemed to accept me from the very beginning. I'd never seen anything like the friendliness among all in that room! Although I'm not positive, I think that was the same day that I met a very friendly Scot named George Johnstone and his American girlfriend, Betsy Messersmith, one of the cutest blondes I'd ever met! The friendliness in that room and George and Betsy changed my life forever.

George for some reason yet to be understood, befriended me, and from then on my success in Scotland was assured. He patiently taught me the ropes, the local customs. For example it was he who taught me that the pubs never required proof of age. For that alone I am indebted to the man forever! Then here was the secret on how to duck out of school if I decided that a pint of bitter at the pub was preferable to a French Class with Wee Nan (Miss Taylor). In fairness, I like to think I might have contributed just a tad to his corruption as well. Like maybe the time we burst out laughing in the back of the room while Mr McAllister was reciting Hamlet's soliloquy scene (at the time of said incident George and I were following the trial of Popinjay in Joseph Heller's *Catch 22*. I supplied the book).

Then there was the episode of the Scottish International Basketball Team. If I remember correctly, the idea was for Northern Ireland, Scotland, England, and Wales to cull their respective grammar schools for a 'national' basketball team, each school providing a player or two. Among others, Dunoon Grammar sent two yanks, Tommy Adams and myself. We were given instructions to take the ferry across to catch the coach that would meet us at such-and-such a time in the early morning that would take us and other team members to Nottingham to play England for our first game the following day.

Tommy and I dutifully arrived at the rendezvous point. And we waited. And we waited. And we waited. No bus arrived. More disturbing to us was the fact that no other team members arrived either. Obviously we had missed the coach.

We didn't know what to do. Going home meant embarrassment and, worse, having to give up missing a couple of authorised days off from school. Then there was also the notion that we might actually be able to help the Scottish team. Well, at least I knew Tommy could. We decided to press on to Nottingham on our own. Out went our thumbs, and sure enough, we were rewarded with a lift that was able to take us just far enough to be left in the middle of nowhere. And so it went throughout the day. Our biggest break was a lift in a coal lorry that really did carry us the bulk of the way, maybe to within about 3 hours of Nottingham. The problem was that it was becoming late evening, and it finally occurred to us that we weren't quite sure where in Nottingham exactly we were supposed to go.

Then an amazing thing happened. Just as we were standing there, a coach went flying by us. Adams, God bless him, recognised a face or two in the window. It was ours! The Scottish team was on that coach merrily on its way to Nottingham! They hadn't seen us, but it was of no matter. A gent in a car was willing to let us jump aboard and off we went in hot pursuit of that beautiful bus, which we pulled up along side about a mile later.

Beautiful Dunoon. My year there was seminal in my life. In fact, this is the perfect opportunity to thank everyone involved. Obviously, besides all of the people who were so kind to me there, and I can't remember one who wasn't, there was the staff of Dunoon Grammar. I mentioned Wee Nan. It was not her fault that I preferred a pub to French class. She tried very hard to help me. Honorable mention has to go to Mr McAllister, who, in spite of my attitude at the time, was able to help me eke out an H level in English. And then there was Mr Blair. I talk about him with reverence even to this day. The way he coaxed an O level grade from me in History is a history-making feat in its own right!

Frank Gonzales was on board the USS *Hunley* in June, 1965

It has been a long time and I may have forgotten many names and places. But what I remember are the enjoyable times in Scotland.

It was a hot summer day in June when I and my family flew from New York to Prestwick Scotland. There was an Air Force Base there. Then a bus ride to Greenock and a boat ride to Dunoon. Besides my wife and I were our three children. Their ages were 2, 1 and 6 months. We had our hands full!

My wife and I are originally from the Philippines and we were used to hot, humid weather. I was in my summer uniform when we left the USA (before Scotland we were in Key West, Florida) and we were not ready for cold weather. Brrrr! We tried to keep the kids warm. Being summertime (?) the hotels were full and we had a difficult time looking for a room. We tried the hotels in Dunoon. We kept trying and ended up in Kilmun. Kilmun Inn had a vacancy so we got settled there. We stayed at the Inn for about 4 weeks till we were able to rent the second floor of a house in Kilmun. At first it was hard for my wife (she was not used to burning coal in the fireplace and did not like the kerosene heater) but after a time we got to love Holy Loch and Scotland.

I was on the USS *Hunley* in Scotland and took her back to the States in 1966.

Jamie is photographed before dancing at Cowal Games

Jamie van Noppen
(née Messersmith)

December 23, 1962 – Arrived at 'Marshill' aged 8. Mrs Riley, our landlady, made our first few weeks very comfortable. A coal fire, comforters on the bed with hot water bottles at the bottom and top and Christmas trifle with sherry! Mr Riley spent most of the day by the panorama window with his binoculars looking out at the spectacular view of the busy River Clyde. He made me feel special and I considered him a grandfather by the end of the three years we lived there.

I loved the playground and the 'guttser' swing down on the West Bay. The Lido was close by and swimming and wading on the rocks. I love rocks to this day! I walked along the back of Kilbride Road, past the Waterworks and the Episcopal Church, over the bridge, by the dairy, then up to the newspaper shop and over to Mary Street Primary School.

I was a year older than my classmates in Primary 3. The work was very structured with lots of effort to be neat. Use of an eraser was to be avoided! I enjoyed sewing and knitting and managed first place awards for two years. I still have the books that were given to me for it. I think the other girls were okay with that. It may have surprised the teachers that a 'Yank' could do that, but they could take credit for the instruction given me. I remember Miss Ferguson, Miss Smith, and Miss Kirkwood.

Was I Catholic or Protestant, Mommy?! The kids said it's very important to know this! Well, up to this point, I had been a Lutheran, but that was confusing to the kids at school and they weren't sure about that answer. Eventually, I decided I wasn't Catholic so that must make me a Protestant!

My friends were Susan Campbell, Margaret McFarlane, Lydia Curran, Fiona and Rosemary, Colin, Andrew. Aden came one year. His dad was in the British Military Service and had come from Yemen.

Mary Street closed and we moved to the old Dunoon Grammar School on Hill Street. The Sweet Shop on Hill Street was fantastic! I remember the covered alley through to the Crescent, called a 'lane'.

Mrs Ayers was Australian by birth and married to an American serviceman. She was a certified dance teacher and held Highland dancing classes on Hunter Street in a church. I took tap and Scottish Highland Dancing. Most of the students were American. The class was invited to dance at the Dunoon Cowal Games and it was very exciting. I passed exams for the Bronze and Silver Medal. I missed the exam for the Gold Medal because my parents took me to London for Sir Winston Churchill's funeral. I remember that event with reverence to a man who was 'history'.

I love the rain. Learning to get through the day walking in rain is what gives you the stamina to have a great day. Looking to the break in the clouds for the sun to make an appearance. Dunoon was a beautiful place to grow up in!

Clara Harrison was the daughter of a serviceman. She and her brother Vic arrived in the early 1960s

I shall never forget the day my dad came home and told us we would be going to Scotland. There was no jumping for joy in our house. Not that day. Being a teenager my first thoughts were 'I can't leave my friends!' and 'But, I'm not that far from graduating! There's no way!' So, immediately, I whined, 'Dad can't we just stay here?' After all, I selfishly reasoned, it wasn't the first time he would be away from home for a long stretch. And, Mom and the three of us Navy brats had managed quite well on our own in his absence. Of course, we all know that didn't happen. Sadly, I gave the news to all my friends and classmates. Then, I managed to live in despondent misery for the next few months as we packed, threw out or donated all the things mom deemed was excess baggage. Her decisions were based on the list dad had brought home with suggestions of things to bring and not to bring to Scotland. We had to find new homes for our pets because dad said the length of time the animals had to be in quarantine would be too hard on them. How on earth would they ever understand we didn't desert them?

Three months later and most thankfully, from my mom's perspective, we arrived at McGuire AFB to fly out. By that time, too, we had all decided to look at this as an opportunity and adventure. Like most of the military dependents we flew via MATS. Not the luxury jetliners of today but a noisy propeller-driven plane which meant a long bone-jarring trip of at least ten hours based on weather and tailwinds.

Our first night in Scotland was spent at Prestwick. Hey, this isn't so very different than the US. Well, a little maybe. Then, the next day our real journey began. Mom, my brother Vic and younger sister, Susan have reminisced so many times about that day. It was as if we had opened a Dickens novel and stepped back in time. A time when life moved at a much slower pace than we were accustomed, a time when people took the necessary moments to visit with friends right there along the way. The three of us teenagers were enchanted by everything we saw – the double decker buses, the narrow cobblestone streets, the sheep grazing peacefully on the hillsides, so many people walking or cycling rather than dashing about in their cars, and the Scottish cows with their long hair. I can clearly recall the first time we heard the lilt and roll of the Scottish brogue quickly followed by our total confusion. Hadn't we been told the Scots spoke the same language as Americans?

Dad had leased a flat on the bottom level of a three storey. And, he said it was fully furnished (truly, the furniture was mostly antiques and was beautiful) and came equipped with all the 'modern' conveniences – central heat and air (ie, there was a fireplace and windows in every room), hot water (ie, if we kept the fire going under the immerser unit), kitchen with all the appliances (a narrow lean-to that had been added on to the flat equipped with a small three burner stove, wooden sink and the fridge was a box that hung on the outside but opened to the inside). Mom completely missed the kitchen when she walked through the apartment despite the fact that she entered the door there.

"I can still feel the bone-chilling coldness
of crawling in between the sheets.
And then, the delightful pleasure of
finding under the covers
the warm brick wrapped in flannel"

Of all of us, Mom had the most adjusting to do. Prior to the trip over she had sold her automatic washer to buy a wringer washer because the electrical current had to be converted through a transformer which was not strong enough to operate the automatic. To her chagrin there were no 'one-stop shop' supermarkets or bag boys to carry the brown paper sacks loaded with a week's worth of groceries out to the car. Instead, she made daily walking trips to town taking a leather bag to bring home the items she would buy at the greengrocers, the meat mongers and the sweet shop to prepare our meals. She learned how to build a coal fire and keep the home fires burning. And how to make our beds warm at night. I can still feel the bone-chilling coldness of crawling in between the sheets. And then, the delightful pleasure of finding under the covers the warm brick wrapped in flannel and placed at the foot of the bed.

How many of you remember the teen club we had at the YMCA and the fun times shared there by American, as well as, Scot teens? It took lots of persuasion and parental support to gain that privilege in a facility built primarily for the sailors. Do you recall the old quonset hut where we held our first teen club meetings? I can laugh now but there was a day when several of us decided to skip school. We had a meeting the evening prior and had managed to leave a window in the back unlatched. The next morning instead of going to school we climbed through the window. We had plans to spend a grand day playing games. It ended up being one of the coldest most miserable days of our lives spent in that old quonset hut. The sinking sick feeling in the pit of my stomach still returns when I think of local workmen who showed up and laboured nearby all the live long day. We didn't dare make a sound for fear of being caught and so stayed huddled together down near some cabinets. That was the first and last time I dared to skip school.

The astonished looks on the locals faces when our 1959 apple-green Ford would 'hog' the narrow streets of Dunoon. The chuckles and laughter that ensued when mom drove through town with the biggest Christmas tree we have ever had tied securely on the top. Being 13 feet it extended beyond both ends of the car. Thanks to teamwork and much huffing and puffing, Mr Sparkenbaugh, Mr Miller and dad were able to get it into our flat. I remember we only had enough ornaments to decorate the front of the tree. But it was breathtaking. My family has made watching the Chevy Chase movie 'A Christmas Vacation' a tradition during the holidays primarily because of the Christmas tree scenes and the memories it triggers.

I was convinced I could still hear the footsteps of all the students who had gone up and down those worn narrow stairs of Dunoon Grammar School for so many years before us. Remember how deep the curve was in them? The sense of history when you found someone's initials and an astonishing old date carved into the wood of the old desks. Kids are still kids no matter the time or place. Then, there was the austere presence of teachers in long black robes and the sameness of having to wear the school uniform. It's a bit moth-eaten but I still have my school blazer. Will any of us forget the fear of the lash from the belt or the belt's

"Will any of us forget the fear
of the lash from the belt
or the belt's exact dimensions?"

exact dimensions? There was the American pride all of us teens shared when Melinda Pigg took several lashes and didn't shed a tear (at least not in public). God bless her! Remember how awful her hand looked for days afterward?

The new sound and shaggy looks of the Beatles. No way they would be a hit in IVY league USA. Oops, we missed that one didn't we?

The frightened and nervous feelings that engulfed our family the day we awoke to discover no ships tendered in the Loch. The Cuba crisis!

The tearful night we heard that President Kennedy had been assassinated. I had been babysitting for Don and Helen Sparkenbaugh. Keith and Lori-Dee were splashing in the bath when the BBC broke into the programme with the dreadful announcement. Amid tears and fears, I hurriedly got the children out of the tub, wrapped them in towels, rushed to the telephone and was one of the first of many to call the YMCA where most of our parents were having an evening out.

The many mornings when I went to wake my brother Vic and would find Keith Carrera, Hammy Martin and Ross McLeod sleeping there, too.

The excitement of the Games, the sound of a thousand plus bagpipes, the skill of the caber tossers, the quick graceful precision of the dancers. Men in kilts (still one of the handsomest sights I've ever seen). My brother, Vic, was a steward an honour he has long remembered with pride.

Cold, misty, grey days. Sparkling clear bright days. The lush green of the fields. The rough craggy rocks and ledges.

It's so easy to relive the wonderful smells of clean fresh air coming off the Clyde, the delicious flavour of Cadbury's Fruit & Nut (still my favorite sweet). And, oh, the aroma and taste of Fish 'n Chips hot from frying and soaked in malt vinegar. Delish delites!

Rushing to meet that special someone who stood quietly and patiently on the corner in a cold drizzling rain waiting for me. The warmth of his smile, the depth of his eyes, the feel of my hand in his, the smell of him, the lift of my heart.

Walks to town, walks in the Fairy Glen and water works, walks along the Promenade. Tender moments.

Cherished friends, wonderful memories, special times all so very, very dear.

The last morning, watching and waving good-bye, the ferry slowly pulling away from the pier taking us far and away, the forlorn sadness, the wrench of leaving a piece of my heart that was torn from me and has remained forever in Scotland. The tears I cried. . . and cried. . . and cried. The promise that someday I would return.

Little America – the hamburger stall at Ardnadam pier became a place to hang out for local youth. It was later converted to a Dunkin' Donuts outlet

Tracy Jackson Heffron came to Scotland in 1962 as a teenager

As the daughter of a Naval officer, I was used to moving around a lot, experiencing new places and friends and coping pretty quickly. We had lived in Connecticut, Maine, Virginia, Puerto Rico and Hawaii, and now we were going to Scotland!

My father went on before us and rented a house in Hunter's Quay. It was a large home, almost twenty rooms, on two and a half acres, overlooking the Holy Loch. When we arrived, he told us the house had been empty for fifteen years, and upon seeing the house inside, my mother started crying. Although it was needing a clean, it was filled with priceless antiques and beautiful carved fireplaces. Our furniture did not arrive for two months and we slept on straw mattresses. Soon, though, we had 'Renfield' cleaned up and ready for my mother's famous cocktail and dinner parties.

When it was time to start school, we had to buy our own uniforms, something we did not wear in America. The first day, all the Americans stood together, while the rest of the students checked us out. We were the very first group of Americans! I had never been in a school so strict, Girls' and Boys' entrances, separate playgrounds, teachers allowed to belt us, lots more schoolwork. It was a little UNNERVING, but I quickly felt right at home, and I loved Scotland and the Scots from the first day.

I soon fell into the routine of a local teenager. On Friday nights, I took Highland dancing lessons and on Saturday nights, it was either the cinema or a dance with my new (first) boyfriend. The dances were wonderful; my favourite was the Scouts' Ball, when all the boys wore their kilts.

After months of dance training, I was ready for the Cowal Games. I'll never forget when the announcer said, 'Tracy Jackson, the only American.'

Everything was so inexpensive then! The bus, pastries, phone, meals, everything for just a few pence.

In the summer of 1963, we were transferred to hot San Diego, California. Friends gave my brother Randy and me a going away party at the Royal Marine Hotel. On the morning we left, people came to see us off at the pier. I think I cried all the way to the West Coast.

To this day, I am amazed at how often I think of Scotland, even after so many years. A rainy day, a certain stone building, someone wearing a tartan outfit – it doesn't take much to bring back memories. It really was a defining time in my life, and I feel so grateful to have experienced the beauty of Scotland and her people.

Slainté Va.

Ralph S Jackson, sr (Tracy's father) was among the first arrivals of high ranking Naval officers to the Base, and had to meet the challenges of pioneers, as did his wife and family

In 1960 USS *George Washington* [SSBN 598], a nuclear propelled submarine equipped with Polaris ballistic nuclear tipped missiles departed Charleston, South Carolina, for the first US Polaris patrol. The submarine's mission was to remain submerged undetected for about 78 days within range of strategic targets to act as a deterrent against possible nuclear attacks against the United States and to be ready to launch missiles against any aggressor nation. At the end of its patrol *George Washington* would proceed to its base being established in Scotland, specifically in the Holy Loch.

While *George Washington* was conducting its first patrol manned by its blue crew, USS *Proteus* [AS19] proceeded to Scotland to its new home port and moored in a body of water named the Holy Loch. It did not moor to a pier on the beach but rather to large mooring buoy anchored in the middle of the Holy Loch. *Proteus's* mission was to serve as a refit and supply ship for SSBNs returning from patrols. SSBNs upon arrival alongside *Proteus* would take on a new crew (Gold being the relief for a Blue crew) and get ready for the next patrol in a period of 21 days. *George Washington* was the first SSBN, but more would come making a total of 10 SSBNs assigned to the organisational command of Commander Submarine

Squadron 14 embarked in *Proteus*. My job on the squadron staff was Chief Staff Officer and Readiness and Operations Officer. I was at that time a Navy Commander. I was also the designated Liaison Officer with the British Navy.

Proteus was met upon its arrival in the Holy Loch by a large number of disruptive protesters mostly from industrial Glasgow across the Firth of Clyde. Many protesters were embarked in small boats trying to block *Proteus's* entry. Some tried to board *Proteus* while others established tent camps ashore. The local police successfully kept the crowds from causing significant problems. The people who lived in the small towns around the Holy Loch were friendly, welcomed the US presence, and took pains to apologise for the Glasgow crowd which was trying to keep the US Navy from carrying out its mission – a mission which had been approved at the highest level of the British government.

Concurrent with *George Washington's* return from its first patrol, its Gold crew arrived having been transported by a large transport plane from the NAS Quonset, RI, to Prestwick AFB in Scotland. The Gold crew took over immediately, and the Blue crew departed by air to its homebase in Groton, CT, to await its turn to return for the next patrol. Meanwhile, the Gold crew took *George Washington* to sea for its second patrol (again for a duration of about 78 days). This started the cycle to be followed by the next nine SSBNs in the squadron. USS *Patrick Henry* [SSBN 599] was the next SSBN to appear.

The refit and supply of submarines, the daily negotiations with the British Admiralty on routine procedures and logistics – all took everyone's time. We worked seven days a week spending very little time ashore enjoying the wonders of Scotland and its countryside.

Uppermost in the minds of the *Proteus* crew and Submarine Squadron 14 staff (both of which were officially homeported in Scotland) was when could officers and enlisted personnel bring their dependents to Scotland. Rules were established to the effect that anyone locating and renting a suitable place would then be authorised to transport family and household effects to Scotland. Right away it became obvious that there were very few places to rent. The surrounding towns (the largest being Dunoon) were small and had for years geared their rentals to accommodating tourists from England and other locations in Scotland mainly in the summer months. Fortunately, the local population decided for the most part to rent to the Yanks rather than the tourist crowds. The result was a wonderful integration of Americans and Scots.

I wasn't having much success in finding a place for my family consisting of my wife, two daughters, and two sons, until one day someone told me about a 'famous' summer home in Hunter's Quay which was available. The original owners were dead and the house had been sold by auction to a person not wealthy enough to maintain it. Unfortunately, it had not been lived in for ten years except when migrating gypsies camped out in the house. The house known as Renfield (all houses had names rather than numbers) consisted of 26 rooms, 3 stories, front and back stairways, and 16 very small and shallow fireplaces. Wallpaper in each room was falling from the ceilings and walls. Lump coal had been dumped in the middle of the kitchen which had no cupboards nor work counters. The entire house was littered with broken and unusable furniture. The grounds were overgrown with tall grass and weeds which made the local sheep happy. Most of the glass panes in a former greenhouse were broken. Tall trees grew in the middle of what used to be a tennis court. The whole place was depressing. However, I kept thinking how grand it must have been in earlier days and decided that with a 'little' hard work it could be made liveable. Accordingly, I rented Renfield for the equivalent of $75 per month with a three-year lease and sent authorisation for my family to move household effects and themselves to Scotland. I was stuck with Renfield, or as my friends described it – 'Jackson's Folly'.

My family arrived by military aircraft at Prestwick AFB where I met them in a normal size squadron automobile since my little Morris Minor could barely seat four. Everyone was full of enthusiasm and could not wait to see Renfield. Chicken that I was, I informed everyone that we were spending the weekend in Edinburgh which was really famous and beautiful. The announcement was met with some disappointment, but everyone humoured to old dad. After Edinburgh, I could not avoid the issue any longer and drove to Renfield in the small village of Hunter's Quay. In preparation for the arrival of my family I had a truck haul away the broken furniture, swept the place, and borrowed eight canvas cots for our beds. Upon approaching Renfield (a 'stately' three storey stone building) there were 'oohs' and 'ahs' and much glee until I opened the front door. The family was shocked and in tears. My wife demanded, 'What have you done – we can't live here'. I calmed things down when I described my plan. Clean the house from top to bottom. Hang new wallpaper. Buy many inexpensive rugs. There were doubts, but the plan was accepted. What other choice? The next day we hired a cleaning lady who worked for two weeks until her back 'gave out'. She became eligible for disability pay. The same was true for succeeding cleaning ladies who would work a few weeks then quit to receive disability pay. Meanwhile, great progress was being made. Things were beginning to look livable, and when our furniture finally arrived (which included a baby grand piano) Renfield became a home.

My children entered the local schools, travelled to school via public bus (very cheap), and adapted rapidly to the new environment. My wife made friends with neighbours, loved Scotland, and somehow managed to survive the cold temperature in our house. Cold temperatures were obvious when the toilet bowls would freeze. My daughters learned Highland dancing and wore kilts when performing. My sons learned to play soccer (called 'football' by the locals) and failed to convince the Scots that baseball was the only real game. I travelled to my sons' rooms on the third floor of Renfield at least once a week to order that they pick up their clothes. The sons also wore the kilt to church and to Boy Scout meetings. No one prescribed which tartan should be worn. The family entertained extensively and became a hangout for various submarine Blue and Gold skippers. We introduced the Scots to charcoal grilled steaks, and they were aghast at our outlandish treatment of cold meat. The family travelled a lot and visited much of Scotland. We went to London and to cities in Europe (in our little Morris Minor). We had the honour of attending three years in a row as guests the Argyll and Sutherland Highlanders Army regimental ball in Stirling Castle (black-tie affair with Scottish dancing until sunrise). My oldest daughter went to France on a school trip for several days speaking only French. Both daughters competed in Highland dancing and did well.

Three years in Scotland went by much too fast. The Scots learned to live with their American visitors, and we learned to live with the Scots who in many ways profited by the US presence (local businesses prospered, landlords made more money, etc). The Scots had a sense of humour and were comfortable friends. It was a great experience for my entire family. Renfield and the Scottish people will always be in our hearts.

Captain Art Bivens had a distinguished Naval career. As a young officer he was part of the first submarine crew exchange on the Holy Loch, in 1961, and returned in 1970 for another tour of duty with his wife Marcy and children, Chrissie, Susie and Jonnie

Transporting the relieving crew from our home port of New London was quite an ordeal in those early days. We were bussed from New London to Maguire Air Force Base in New Jersey where our crew of 140 officers and men was divided into two groups to fly two prop planes under contract to the US Air Force. All the various ratings and specialists were carefully divided in case one of the planes went down. Happily we never lost a plane in the thirty years of flying. The two-plane airlift was abandoned with the advent of the larger and more reliable jet airliners. On the early flights, the planes landed in Gander, Newfoundland to refuel for the final push across the Atlantic.

Our first impression of Scotland in March 1961 was of the typically gloomy and misty day, not one to heighten our spirits. We landed at Prestwick where we were in for another long bus ride. At the time few of us appreciated the fact that we were in the heart of Robbie Burns' country, or that we were right next to the famous British Open golf courses of Troon, Turnberry and Prestwick. Not until later did I come to understand and appreciate Scotland better. At Greenock we again had to load ourselves, our luggage and crew records into several boats for the thirty minute ride across the Clyde to the Holy Loch and the *Proteus*.

No one was sure how long a proper crew turnover should take. Some people said it should be two weeks with both crews working together to help speed the refit. Our first one there was ten days and that was too long. The off-going crew was eager to go home and the on-coming crew did not want them around after a few days because the 'ownership' role had changed too. Soon after this initial crew exchange the overseas turnover length stabilised at four days.

In addition to the *Proteus* and the Gold Crew, the *Patrick Henry's* entry into the Holy Loch was enlivened by greeters who were not exactly friendly to our presence. Hundreds of anti-nuclear demonstrators were on hand, along with the press, to complicate the crew relief. Some of the demonstrators paddled out in kayaks to harass or even board the ship. We had to develop new procedures to handle this kind of activity. Our Repel Boarders Bill was too violent and deadly for demonstrators. We warned the demonstrators not to touch the ship and if they climbed aboard we were instructed to take them into custody and then hand them over to the British Constabulary. We also greased the top our upper rudder to foil attempts to climb up and perch on it. The majority of the demonstrators sat down outside the gate to the British government pier at Ardnadam and tried to block access. The British constables were quite efficient and the demonstrators were mostly peaceful, most of them sitting and shouting 'No Polaris' as we picked our way through them, either going ashore or returning to the ship.

(Note: One of the demonstrators, an avowed Communist, later was a Maths teacher for one of my children, in the local school.)

The Holy Loch thus became our first overseas refit base for an FBM submarine squadron.

The Holy Loch, the Firth of Clyde and the surrounding Scottish country is remarkably beautiful and enchanting. Many people are put off at first by the rainy weather and the short winter days. Some of our sailors griped that the beer in the local bars was served at room temperature and that the bars closed at 10:00pm. Also, we had to time carefully our evenings ashore with the liberty boat schedule. But for those who took the time to explore the country and got to know the local people, or lived there as I did later with my family while on the squadron staff, Scotland was a wonderful experience.

In 1970 I had been picked to be the first Training and Readiness officer of Submarine Squadron14 in Holy Loch, Scotland. For the previous ten years there had been no Training Officers for SSBN squadrons because these early FBM submarines had experienced officers and crew, and the commanding officers had previously had submarine command. But as the numbers of FBM submarines increased, the experience level of the officers and crew decreased significantly. In 1960 all officers on the early SSBNs were qualified submariners from diesel boats and most also had surface ship experience. By 1970 all the officers reporting aboard, below department head were fresh out of the Naval Academy or NROTC. Even

the submarine school course had been reduced from 6 months to 6 weeks in length. What really triggered the need for a training and readiness officer for each squadron was when SSBNs started failing their operational reactor safeguards examination. Also, about one fourth of the crew was transferred off after each patrol and the replacements needed to be trained to become an intregal part of the ship's organisation.

We flew into Prestwick, on a gloomy November day where we were met by a driver and a Navy van. He drove us to Greenock where Commander Chuck Tate and his wife Sharon met us with a navy launch. We then embarked for a thirty minute ride to the Holy Loch on the opposite side of the Firth. It was dark and rainy when we arrived at the Ardnadam pier. At 56^0N latitude darkness comes early in November. It was not a pleasant beginning for our Scottish tour of duty. But Chuck and Sharon were pleasant and welcoming and stayed with us for our final ride of the day to the 'Balmoral House' in Dunoon, a Bed and Breakfast inn run by the O'Neals. This would be our home for the next six weeks until our furniture arrived and we could move into Newton Linn.

The biggest problem at Balmoral House was staying warm. Our bedroom and the girls' bedroom each had an electric heater attached to the wall that required one to feed it shillings to get heat. It was ten minutes per shilling and I was always running out of them. The lounge was kept warm though, so we spent our evenings drinking inexpensive Portuguese Mateus wine and chatting with the other guests. We had the use of the kitchen and shared the stove with the other guests for the evening meals. The O'Neals were wonderful people and introduced us to Scottish life and their friends and gave us a truly warm reception. We went to several Scottish dances (ceilidhs in Gaelic) during that time and learned some of the Scottish dances such as the 'Gay Gordons'. Great fun! There was drinking at these dances and the Brits are very strict about drinking and driving, so we always took a taxi.

Commander Chuck Tate, the squadron Chief Staff Officer, got the job of finding us a place to live. Chuck and Sharon Tate had a cleaning lady, Mrs Mac (McLaughlan), who knew of an available place. It was a two storey, four bedroom flat in Innellan. It was one of four flats in an old Scottish mansion called 'Newton Linn'. It was owned by David Boyd, a rather famous yachtsman who designed the 12 metre yacht *Sceptre*, the British challenger for the first Americas Cup series held after World War II, built in Sandbank.

Newto Linn was built in 1852 for a wealthy leather merchant from Glasgow. It had beautiful grounds facing the Firth of Clyde. A gardener, Mr Campbell, kept the flowers and gardens looking lovely for a very modest fee. Mrs Mac came once a week to clean. She charged one pound and wouldn't take any more. She was more a visiting friend than a servant.

There was no central heating so we kept warm with two paraffin heaters and several electric heaters scattered about. The standard household electric current was 220 volts so we had to use transformers (220 to 110v) for our American appliances. We had to rent a TV because American sets don't work in Britain. However, the inconveniences were minor considering we probably had one of the nicest homes available in the area. It would be our home for the next two years and we grew to love the place.

The one thing that wasn't cheap was electricity. We got the bill once a quarter and it was always a big one, especially in the winter. For several months during one winter the coal miners and power plant operators were on strike and we had rolling blackouts. It seemed we were always blacked out in the hours of 6-12pm; no lights, no 'telly', no heat.

Until our car arrived I rented an English Ford to get around in and drive to work. It was about seven miles to Ardnadam on the Holy Loch where I took a five minute boat ride to the tender moored to a buoy in the middle of the loch. I had to get used to shifting gears with my left hand and driving on the left side of the road.

With the arrival of our furniture and car we moved to our flat in Newton Linn. We never worried about our kids. They could catch the bus to Dunoon from a stop on the Shore Road just outside the gate. Or they could take the bus beyond Dunoon out to Ardnadam where we had a small support establishment for our submarine squadron. They had a lot of freedom and soon developed a lot of Scottish and American friends.

Another hangout was the combination YMCA/USO facility in Dunoon, which was available for our young sailors and dependents. Among the activities provided was Saturday afternoon movies. At that time there

The American Years

were a series of British comedies with 'Carry On' in the title. Susie was there one day for the showing of 'Carry On Camping'. The room was full of dependents and children. It turned out that the movie was about a nudist colony and soon after it started it showed a naked man and woman walking out of a tent. The kids were titillated, but the shocked adult supervisors had the movie stopped forthwith. On another occasion I walked into the YMCA looking for Susie. I spotted her before she saw me. She was sitting on a table chatting with a couple of sailors and smoking a cigarette. When she saw me she practically choked on that cigarette. She was 13 or 14 at the time.

Susie got caught smoking but I never caught Chrissie in the act. I didn't find out until years later that the three elderly sisters living in one of the downstairs flats lead her 'astray'. Frances and Ailene Malloy, and their elder sister, Mrs McLennon, liked Chrissy who was about 16 at the time. They would lure her into their flat to have a cigarette and a chat. They obviously enjoyed the younger American company. We were fond of the three sisters.

Of the other residents of Newton Linn, Mr and Mrs Wilson lived in the flat directly below our flat. Mr Wilson was a retired mining engineer who had spent many years in Spain. He was like many Scots we met who had worked all over the world, mostly in the British Empire, then came home to retire when their work was done, or as a result of the shrinking of the Empire. The Wilsons were very kind to us.

In addition to helping the SSBNs in Submarine

Squadron 14 with their training and readiness I had to help the resident submarine tender, USS *Canopus*, get well. The ship was in trouble with Admiral Rickover, having failed its Radiological Safety Examination. The tender was not immune from close scrutiny. She provided radiological support services, such as taking aboard radioactive coolant water and solid radioactive waste from from SSBNs alongside.

When a nuclear submarine starts up its reactor the coolant water heats up and expands. In the early days of operating these nuclear plants we simply discharged this water into the surrounding water and figured it was harmless because of the dilution effect. However, the British authorities called us on that assertion when they took bottom core samples underneath the tender in the Holy Loch and the samples turned out to contain minute corrosion particles of radioactive cobalt 60. No more coolant discharges into the loch or any other body of water within twelve miles of a shoreline. Divers from the tender now had to hook up a gooseneck pipe and hose to the underwater discharge port on the submarine. The coolant water would then be discharged to the radioactive holding tanks in the tender. From then on even a teacup of leakage into the loch was a sin and subject to penalty. But the radioactive waste couldn't stay on the tender indefinitely.

The tender got underway every three months to prove that she was still a sea going vessel. During this time at sea she would discharge the radioactive liquid waste into deep ocean areas distant from any shores. The solid waste such as contaminated rags, tape, and rubber gloves were compacted into 55 gallon drums for later shipment back to the US. If the tender screwed up in operating any of their radioactive systems or messed up their record keeping, especially during an inspection they were decertified to perform radioactive procedures. That's where I came in. Again, just like a submarine that had failed an ORSE, when a radioactive procedure was to be perfomed I had to station myself in the tender's radioactive processing system spaces and oversee the valve lineups and insure that proper procedures were followed meticulously. This continued for several weeks until the tender passed a re-exam and was re-certified.

I was also involved in at least one major radioactive emergency exercise that extended beyond the confines of the *Canopus* to the entire Holy Loch area. An earlier exercise of this size had been conducted before I arrived. The tender had sent their radioactive detection teams ashore in full anti-contamination clothing and equipment. When the locals saw these people roaming around they became alarmed that there was a true emergency and that they were being zapped with radiation. So, to allay such fears this time and without making a big announcement of the exercise to the local community we did not send any of the teams ashore or conduct any overt activity that would unduly arouse the locals.

Meanwhile Chrissie and Susie attended Dunoon Grammar School. They caught the public bus to school just outside the gate to Newton Linn. At school all the kids wore a uniform. This was a great equaliser for teenagers. Jon's little Innellan school did not require

uniform. Chrissie finished her 10th grade and took her O-levels and passed. She needed some American school credits for our colleges, so at the beginning of her 11th grade she transferred to our American school at High Wycombe Air Force Base. Susie continued on at Dunoon Grammar School in the 8th grade.

Marcy and I were often invited to Saturday night dances sponsored by various groups and held at such Dunoon landmarks as the Queen's Hall and McColl's Hotel. They included the Banker's Ball, the Policemen's Ball, the Golf Club Ball and others. The dance floor at the McColl's Hotel was particularly nice. It moved up and down on springs. At these dances, or ceilidhs, the couples danced in a counter clockwise circle to choreographed routines that the Scots all seemed to know. A few titles include 'Strip the Willow', the 'Canadian Barn Dance' and the 'Gay Gordons'.

We didn't have to go to Turnberry or St Andrews to enjoy great Scottish golf. For five shillings we could play the local Cowal Golf Course. The view from those fairways on the hills above Dunoon provided such a beautiful panorama of the Firth of Clyde that it was difficult to concentrate on hitting the ball. On the Cowal course and the other smaller nine hole courses near Dunoon we had to play through the sheep which were allowed to roam and graze where they pleased. The Dunoon Rotary Club always invited the senior navy officers to their annual Burns Night in January, at which there was much drinking of whisky, reciting Burns unintelligible poetry, and trying to get down that awful tasting haggis!

After two years in Scotland I was ready for a change of pace. Marcy and the children would have liked to have stayed for another year and looking back it probably would have been better for the children's education. However, those two years in Scotland were at a time that they treasure. The children were of an age that they could assimilate and take advantage of the opportunity to broaden their education and outlook on a slightly different culture. We all look back on those two years as a wonderful experience.

These are extracts from Art Bivens's book 'Of Nukes and Nosecones' and his forthcoming autobiography.

Brad McDonald's father was an Officer on board the third ship sent to Holy Loch

My journey to the land of kilts, bagpipes and 'paraffin' heaters began in September 1966 when my father was ordered to the grand ship USS *Simon Lake*, which was located in Holy Loch, Scotland. I was eleven years old and my sisters were seven and thirteen. We travelled from our home in Washington DC by car, bus, taxi, ocean liner, train, ferry; you name it, everything but an airplane; and finally, via New York, Southampton, London, Glasgow, and Gourock, ended up at the Royal Marine Hotel on the 'Low Road', which wound around Holy Loch.

From our hotel we could see the American submarine haven – the 'tender' (mother ship), several submarines, the dry-dock and the hustle bustle of small boats running back and forth from the piers at Ardanadam and Kilmun, transporting American sailors to and from their ships. To me it was an absolutely majestic site. In retrospect, I can easily see why the locals viewed it as an absolute invasion of their quiet, humble lifestyle, one that until the early '60s seemed to have been relatively untouched by the modern world.

After a month at the Royal Marine, a time in which we were introduced to scones, shortbread, fish and chips, afternoon tea and loaves of unsliced bread fresh from the bakery (the best thing since sliced bread!), we moved into our home – Polmarlach, just three houses down from the Strone House, on the edge of

Blairmore. Then I learned about coal stoves, paraffin heaters and 'transformers'. Those of us spoiled Americans who grew up with central heating spent a good bit of our time trying to stay warm. But it was sort of fun, stoking the 'Rayburn' stove with coal before bedtime, so there would be just a glimmer of hot coals in the morning, enough to get the fire going for breakfast. In the morning my dad would just immediately head for the ship, where he knew he could get a long, hot shower and all the hot coffee he wanted. My Mom and sisters and I would huddle around the Rayburn for some heat.

Shortly after our arrival in Scotland, my father was invited to a grand gathering of the McDonald clan in Glasgow. Being as my father was a fairly senior officer, and a McDonald, he was asked to give some brief remarks at the banquet. He arrived with notes in hand, arrayed in his formal dinner dress uniform. He planned to talk about how he had brought two great Scottish clans together, by marrying a Campbell. Upon arrival at the door he was greeted by an elderly, bearded, kilted man who said, in his deep Scottish brogue, 'Ye've probly ne'er been to one of our gaherins; just one word of advice – DON'T MENTION THE WORD CAMPBELL!' Dad calmly threw his notes in the closest waste bin and quickly changed his remarks. Little did he know that this wise move saved him a lot of embarrassment, and possibly his life.

The following week my mother was enrolling my younger sister in Kilmun Primary School. The headmaster laughed when he read her name – Sheila Campbell McDonald. He explained to my mother the long standing feud between the Campbells and McDonalds and how to that day there was still distrust. This was the first we had heard of the feud and it was now clear that my father had narrowly avoided major trouble at the McDonald gathering in Glasgow!

My older sister and I took the bus every morning, from Blairmore, around the Holy Loch and into Dunoon, where we attended Dunoon Grammar School (DGS). There was a group of perhaps 40-50 American teens of which we were part. We had to stick together, for camaraderie and occasionally for mental and physical protection. The Scottish youth had widely varying attitudes towards us, everything from downright friendliness and a few teenage romances to outright hostility and violence. I got accustomed to spending most of my time at DGS looking behind my back and wondering where the next punch, shove, kick or trip would come from. At lunchtime I would do my best to leave the school campus and walk into Dunoon. I figured the less time I spent outside of classroom on campus, the less chance I had of getting mugged.

To this day I clearly remember frequently stopping by a small candy shop a few blocks from school. The owner was a kind, elderly gentleman who was always delighted to see me – hey, I was there to buy candy! (or 'sweets' as I learned to call it). His charming little wife was always there with him. The store was tiny and it was wall to wall 'sweets'. The old man proudly announced to me one day that he had a firm handle on the inventory of the store – the total value was three hundred and twelve pounds, eleven shillings and seven pence. It was his life's work, perhaps about $750 worth of candy, a humble store no bigger than a small bedroom, and he and his wife making lots of young folks happy every day – ahhh, for the simpler pleasures of life. For 37 years I have looked back and thought – 'There's a guy who found the true success and happiness of life.'

My second year in Scotland saw me off to Kiel School for Boys, in Dunbarton. I was too young for the American High School in England, but really wanted to get away from the hostility of DGS. (Believe me, I have never held any animosity towards the folks at DGS or anybody else over there who did not openly accept me or my fellow Americans. In fact I think it is remarkable that they put up with us at all. The negative voices and the physical harassment probably originated from a proportionally small minority of residents. And, as I alluded to previously, years later I could easily see how the US presence, our big ships, our nuclear missiles and the almighty dollar forever changed the peaceful way of life the locals had experienced for centuries. Overall, the positive relationships and experiences, in the long run, vastly outweighed the negatives. But it was not easy to see that at the tender age of 12, when my biggest daily concern was to not get beat up or kicked in the head.) So, the only option was to head off to Boarding School! My mother took me to Glasgow to get outfitted with the proper uniforms – including a KILT! – which I still own, although it is a BIT TIGHT around the waist now!

Then I reported into Kiel School, Fall of 1967, as a 'First Year' student. There I learned to play rugby and cricket. I learned to live in close quarters – locker, bunk, locker, bunk, locker, bunk – twenty four of us First Year boys in one dorm room. Everything I had, had to fit into one small locker.

There was much less hostility towards me as an American at Keil School, because the boys were from all over Scotland, and had felt no impact in their families' lives from the presence of the Americans in Holy Loch. But that by no means provided for a tranquil existence. This was the old-fashioned British boarding school at its best. One's best defence was his ability to fight or else his ability to scare others with his size. Fortunately for me I was by far the biggest boy in my class, as big as many of the 16 and 17 year old boys. But I still had my share of brawls. I learned that respect was gained by hitting back, not through appeasement.

Now, after all that, I must say that in retrospect, despite some homesickness, I learned to love Kiel School. I excelled on the rugby team, did very well in academics and made some good friends. We sailed on the River Clyde, travelled to other boarding schools to play their rugby and cricket teams, and survived the nasty hurricane of 1968 together – cleaning up the school grounds of felled trees and other debris from that terrifying nightlong storm. Kiel School did not hire anybody to do that kind of work, it was just us boys! I developed my lifelong passion for tea there (the Scottish boys taught me to stoke up the tea with lots of sugar and cream each morning at breakfast). And I guess I learned that sometimes, the only person that is going to bail me out of a bad situation is – me.

In June of 1968, my parents attended the end of year ceremonies at Kiel School – where I was recognised as the second place student (academically) of the First Year Boys. This recognition included the fact that I was an American and was returning to the United States that summer. I still remember the warm round of applause that the boys and their families gave me. My parents were quite proud too. I clearly remember the car ride back to Holy Loch. We talked about returning to the US and what a great, although difficult, experience Kiel School had been for me. I was so excited to be thinking of returning 'home'.

Now, 35 years later, I think often of returning to Scotland, revisiting Dunoon Grammar School, Kiel School, the Royal Marine Hotel. How about some fish and chips – do they still wrap them in newspaper? I doubt it. How about a trip to the bakery for some fresh UNSLICED bread? I've heard that the North Sea oil business has taken over, no sign of the Americans and their nuclear submarines anymore.

Do you think the old man and his candy store will still be there? I imagine he's long gone – he'd be well over one hundred years old now. But I'd like to see if I can find that SWEET Store anyway, if I do, I know I'll see him there; he and his wife, doling out smiles and confectionaries to young boys and girls on break from Dunoon Grammar School.

Walt Cantrell was stationed at Holy Loch in the early seventies. He brought his wife Betsy and young family with him

Living in Scotland was a true highlight for us – probably our favorite place to live during my husband's 37-year Navy career.

We lived in Burnlea Cottage in the wee village of Clachaig on the road to Colintriave in 1974-75. Initially we were a bit deterred as we adjusted to the absence of central heating (in the precarious days of coal strikes) and our water tumbled down the hillside in a peaty little burn (or failed to make the trip and deserted us), and although the sheep managed to devour every flower I planted, we absolutely loved our quiet remote location.

Our two children, then 6 and 9 years old, went to the wonderful Sandbank School where Miss Renny and Mr Parlane gave them first-class instruction. Our daughter, after a visit to the Cowal Games, wanted to take up Highland dancing and did so with surprising success, taking lessons and being encouraged by Mrs Angus. We had the opportunity to take our small dancer to a number of competitions around Scotland and met lovely people who seemed pleased that a little American wanted to and could dance. The soccer skills our son acquired by playing with school mates continued with him and carried him through college.

We have dozens of fond memories of the special people and beautiful places in Scotland – especially those in the general Dunoon area. My husband, who was Repair Officer in the USS *Canopus*, has always pronounced that his most satisfying job ever. To this day, when we visit a particularly scenic place, we often say, 'Doesn't this remind you of Scotland?'

Bud Fisher worked at the American housing complexes. He and his wife made lifelong friends of Americans

To be honest I wish the Americans were still here. I had a lot of good friends that my wife and I still keep in contact with. I worked doing the maintenance at Waverley Court and Eagle Court, the American housing, so I got to meet quite a lot in my twelve years between 75-87. I also captained the C.P.O. in the local league at darts in which we were beaten finalist in two cups and the best we ever did was third place in the A division. We had such a great bunch of guys that if bodies were required we would all pitch in to help. On one occasion I could not make it to a cup knock-out because I was painting the outside of my house, so the week before the cup games no less than ten of our team turned up to paint so that I could play in the cup the following week. That was one of our beaten finals and all the wives and girlfriends also came along and we had a BBQ which lasted all weekend.

Once the ladies from the wives club had no baby sitter so 'S', a Waverley Court tenant said she would look after them, all 6! I was working in the house repairing cabinet doors and to cut a long story short all 6 required their nappies (diapers) changed at the same time so I offered some help which she was glad of. So 'S' changed 3 and I changed 3. The result being she wrote to my boss to say in all the Navy housing she had stayed in, the workmen would never have changed nappies, so as a wee joke in my tool kit I always had a spare couple of DIAPERS! I got a nice letter of thanks!

Bud Fisher enjoying the American way of life

When my wife, Cathie played darts in the C.P.O. mixed doubles league we were drawn against a Chief called Tom and his wife Meg in a knock-out tournament which Cathie and I won. We sat after the game to have a sociable drink and chat and it turned out that Tom went to school here at the same time as me – his Dad had also been stationed in Dunoon in the sixties. We went through teachers' nicknames as if it were yesterday and locals' names as well. It turned out a cracking night. His name is Tom Fontana.

I was just sitting talking to my wife about some of the Americans that we knew and we spoke about how we met the Esches. We are friendly with Master Chief John Wright and his family, so when John went back to the States, Memphis, one of his Chiefs was Bill Esch, and Bill told John that he was coming to Holy Loch so John told Bill to go by the Queens Hotel and say hi to Bud Fisher which he did. One night I was in the Queens and this big American came in asking where he could find Bud Fisher and one of the locals pointed me out. Bill introduced himself and we have kept in contact ever since. That was 1980-81. We also have been out to the States to visit them in San Diego for a month and we needed a rest when we got back to Dunoon as we were on the go the whole month from Disney World to Sea World and over the border to Mexico. While at Sea World Cathie got to kiss Shamo the killer whale and some years later Shamo died so I said to her, see the effect that you have on kissing (joke) and to this day the Esches and Fishers still keep in touch.

We still keep in touch and when the Navy held its reunion no less than four couples came down to visit and one even had his hip flask that was a going away present.

Vinal C R eynolds was a young sailor on the USS *Holland* in 1975

About a week ago, on a Saturday morning, I looked for a website that might have pictures of Dunoon, Scotland. I was surprised and delighted to find the site that Jim Collins at Thistle Group is working with. You can't imagine the flood of memories that came with finding that sight.

I made the crossing to Scotland from Norfolk, Virginia on board the USS *Holland* AS-32, in November of 1975. We entered the Holy Loch on a beautiful evening just as it was becoming dark. One of my shipmates had been to Scotland on a previous tour and had learned to play the pipes. He was out on deck playing a traditional Scottish song as the ship made its way slowly into the Loch. It is a moment that stands out, not only in my twenty year Navy career, but also in my life.

My wife, Joyce, and our four children joined me in March of the following Spring. Initially we stayed in a B&B called the Ardtully. It was a very old stone home overlooking the loch.

We were treated more like house guests rather than customers. I remember the breakfasts of porridge and toast, dinners of lamb etc. and evenings in front of the fire in the sitting room.

My children all attended local schools and we found them to be excellent.

Mary Lou Branson, Fort Worth, Texas

I got to Scotland after a long plane ride via England as a result of a foul-up in the USA by the US Navy which sent me, instead of flying straight in as I could have done. There was a double rainbow when I landed. I loved the people and they were very, very friendly. I miss them all. I enjoyed that wonderful feeling of acceptance for the two years that I was there.

I loved the food, the friendliness, the pubs, and the country. I kept seeing my McDonald mother in the tearooms. She would have loved it, as I did. I adored living there and would live there again with no problem, except that I also have friends and family here in the USA.

I was the white-haired lady doctor who lived in Jimmy Smart's house in Dunoon and dated one of their own – that was very, very special for me. I marvelled at the weather and thought it kept everything green, as it certainly does. It was a wonderful part of my life that I would not change ever. Love Scotland and all that entails.

John F Mohr, one of the first US Navy arrivals

I arrived with the USS *Proteus* in about early March 1961. How cold it was and the heavy fog that I could see around the land before we got into Holy Loch.

The people were very nice and friendly. I enjoyed meeting all those that I met while in Scotland. I arrived as a SN (E-3). I soon got an apartment and my wife came over shortly after we arrived. I lived in three different apartments while there. I enjoyed the area after I got used to being there and often went to the movie down town Dunoon. I remember riding the double decker bus to town and riding along the winding road with the stone wall. I remember the locals being in swimming when we went by. I remember eating the fish and chips in Dunoon. I often rode the ferry across to Greenock and taking the train to Glasgow. I left Holy Loch in late May of 1962 at the end of my enlistment as RM3.

I still have a lot of memories of my time in the Holy Loch area and would love to be able to return there for a visit some day, but I am 61 years old and have had many health problems and don't think I could make the trip now. I am retired from the Naval Reserve.

Jan Peros

I was stationed in Holy Loch from 1963 to April 1966.

I was a young man, 18 years old, apprehensive, not quite sure what to expect.

I found the people very friendly – difficult to understand – took me WEEKS to get the 'ear'.

I thought the CND demonstrations were strange, at first. I was part of the USS *Hunley* boat crew. . . part of our job was to prevent some of the Committee's demonstrators from reaching and boarding our ship. If, however, they fell (or were tipped) into the Loch, we were to 'retrieve' them and bring them on board to our medical facility.

I spent three years in Scotland. Like most young men, I missed my home and longed to return. Sometimes I felt like the 'Ugly American'. At other times I felt a deep love for the people, customs and countryside. Honestly, there are some things I am proud of, and some things I'm not so proud of regarding my behaviour in Scotland, more of the former than the latter, I like to think. I remember eating far too many scones, and drinking far too many pots of tea on the ferry from Greenock to Dunoon. How impolite, greedy – what the locals must have thought!

Looking back, I see some of the hard times some Scots were going through. After all, the mid-1960s were not that far away from the end of WWII. To me, as a young man, it probably seemed an eternity.

Mini-skirts were in fashion in Great Britain long before they were in America. I remember seeing the young Scots girls very red knees (and pretty legs) and wondering why they were so red. It wasn't long before finding out it was the result of sitting in front of the peat or coal fire, or the 15 minutes worth of electirc heat a shilling might purchase. I was used to central heating in America. It was a mystery to me.

The Scots are a great and generous people – despite the sterotypes the world loves to create!

Allan Porchetta was a Grammar School pupil when the Base arrived

I remember there was quite a lot of interest and excitement about what the Americans would be like. This was because not a lot happened in Dunoon in those days and we were finally in the news.

The Americans who arrived at school were placed in classes where they were about one or two years older than us since at that time we were ahead of them syllabus wise. They were well travelled compared to the average Dunoon pupil – (I had been to Glasgow for the day and Carradale for a week!) – most of the Americans had been around the world in the various American bases that existed at that time. So this made them appear almost brash to many of us. This brashness sometimes got them into trouble with certain teachers in this era of strict classroom discipline.

But on the whole integration took place quickly – probably much more quickly in the school than in the adult world. Although the school uniform was compulsory the Americans had their own variations – such as white bobby socks – which some of the locals started wearing. The Americans often brought their schoolbooks in a poly bag so the locals just had to discard their khaki ex-army soldier bags and follow suit. There were many small culture and fashion changes which were absorbed. I can remember Joe Dallas the PT teacher introducing more basketball and even baseball to accomodate the new arrivals who were not very good at football.

In the adult arena there were lots of sailors walking about in uniforms and a great growth in taxi use. Many of the sailors were looking for 'gals' either local or from further afield in places such as Greenock, Port Glasgow or Glasgow. There would often be trouble between local young men and the 'Yanks' especially if the local talent was seen to be going over to the other side. More pubs and clubs opened up and at a time when being out to 11o'clock seemed late to a local, these sailors would think nothing of returning to base at dawn. Many of the locals were slowly drawn into this late night culture and you could get a hamburger at Mr Urquhart's hamburger stall at 2am outside the Holy Loch pier – this was really living on the wild side in the early sixties!

When the submariners came ashore after being months at sea they went almost wild in the pubs— downing pints of mixed drinks such as the 'Dolphin' in one go. So sometimes the town had a wild west look – especially on a Saturday night when the locals joined in. That's another thing – because the US Navy worked a shift system even a wet Monday night could like a Saturday night especially in pubs like the Argyll. There is no doubt that all this had an effect on local culture and increased consumption of alcohol. The price that Americans could buy drink was almost as cheap as our lemonade so the drink flowed cheaply for some locals who joined in.

Brian L Stewart was returning to his family's roots when he was sent to Holy Loch

I could write a whole book myself about my impressions of Scotland and my time there. In short, I loved it and would love to visit again and bring my family. As a Stewart it was a thrill that if I was to be sent to any other country it would be Scotland. That was truly a dream come true.

My family had come over from Scotland to Nova Scotia and then down through Maine to the Boston Massachusetts area like many other families. This would have been on both my mother's and father's side but in the late 1800s and early 1900s. So, as a Stewart, I was especially proud to visit the homeland.

I was attached to the USS *Alexander Hamilton* from 1982 to 1986 and flew from New London Connecticut to Prestwick in a cycle of 110 days, assigned to the submarine, and 90 days at home. So, you can see that Scotland, or more properly the submarine, was more of my home than the States during this time. I don't remember the season when we arrived in Prestwick for the bus ride to Dunoon but everything was in bloom and my first impression was how neat and quaint everything was. It appeared as though you had just painted everything just for us. Of course, it was very tidy there but the glistening was from a fresh coat of rain, not paint!

In the period of time that most submarine sailors were there, we were generally working on the ship except for some fleeting hours stolen away to town.

Most of my Navy brethren wanted to head for the nearest pub and I often joined them there but I wasn't going to miss some of the local countryside. I took the trip up to see the Queen's reindeer, over to Gourock and Greenock several times and a trip to Glasgow. I saw the Cowal Games and was invited by a family to enjoy a beer in the street. The father had commented on what a fine wool jacket I had on and a plaid, no less and when he found out I was a Stewart, well, they treated me like the Royalty that I never felt I was in the States. He pointed out the Stewart tartan and the musicians and people marching behind them and through the streets of Dunoon at the end of the Games and told me it was a tradition to march behind your tartan. Well, we marched and occasionally stopped at pubs and had a nip and headed back to keep marching. I never had so much fun.

I remember the policewomen you had there. There was an elderly but very fit and able woman who was patrolling the streets one day and she took notice of some kids that were spitting and leaving candy wrappers on the sidewalk and she grabbed an ear or two and had them picking things up straight away! It was great. No lawsuits about police brutality as I recall either. Just a simple 'Yes, Ma'am' from the boys.

Another time I was in a candy store, on the back street, near the monument at the crest of a hill. The monument, as I recall, was to the memory of hundreds of Dunoon villagers years before slaughtered by Campbells. There were jars and jars of candy and I wanted to load up with some to last the next two months while we were under the sea. I was wearing my plaid jacket since it had served me so well on previous visits and the ladies at the counter were offering us free samples and asking us where we were from and our names. Once again I was given the Royal treatment when they found out I was a Stewart but my friends who had Irish names were firmly but politely refused anymore free samples! I told them THAT was the luck of the Irish. They should have been born a Scot!

At the pub across the street on another visit I was enjoying Stewart's Cream of the Barley, compliments of the bartender, when a man walked in with his dog. This would sound like a typical joke if I hadn't been there. Actually, I didn't see the dog as he was a small, black dog and he sat at his master's feet on the floor next to me at the bar, where we were seated. We enjoyed our drinks and after a time I was suddenly aware of the dog because he started barking and the man said 'Okay, okay we can go now.' I thought it was a joke on the Yank but the bartender tells me that the dog knows when he's had his two drinks and then it's time to get back to his wife at home. I can't see any other explanation for that dog's behaviour so I'm a believer. Owning three dogs myself I do know about some of their uncanny abilities. My judgment and clarity could have been affected by the drink. I found a bottle of Stewarts Cream of the Barley at the duty-free shop at the airport and savoured it for some time but I haven't seen it in a shop, since.

The single malt Scotches were a treat I enjoy to this day. As is my love of the Highland games which I had never attended before. The mackerel wrapped in newspaper at the fish and chip stands were a treasure. The little cans of Schweppes tonic on the ferry and the smell of peat being burned and the narrow roads and the taxi drivers pining for a trophy as they rattled us around Dunoon, are memories I'll always hold.

It was a pleasure and a joy to be there and be treated as well as we were. Or, at least, as I was. I don't remember anyone getting the cold shoulder that didn't offer it first. My plaid jacket and (almost) Royal name made that a truly magical place for the short time I was there. When Scotland achieved a measure of independence with the 1998 Scotland Act I was at a Highland Games in New Hampshire when the news broke. The cheering was long and loud there. You would have been proud and so were we. Maybe I raised a sword or two in past lives or fought with Bonnie Prince Charlie at Culloden, I don't know. But I was as proud then as at any of America's celebrations. Maybe more so. It was a long time coming.

If you have the pleasure to speak to the locals there in Dunoon please let them know they did this sailor's heart good.

Patrick McLaughlin EMFA/FN
(then) (USAF retired)

I first arrived in Scotland's Prestwick Airport in September 1975. I was in dress blues with my seabag and orders. I was reporting to my first ship after three months in electrical school followed by two weeks schooling in International Relations which was to prepare you for being home-ported overseas.

Fortunately, for me, a crew member was there to drop off a couple of transferring crew and I came in on the plane they were leaving on. I said fortunately, as I had no idea where I was in relation to where the ship was, much less any knowledge in how to get from point A to point B. (I was excited about being there as I had gotten my first choice – Scotland.)

I knew there would be huge differences and was eagerly waiting to see what they would be. My first shock was approaching the car at the (US) passenger side and seeing a steering wheel. 'Oh, yeah,' I thought. 'The vehicle situation and the road travel direction is reversed.' Let me tell you, knowing the travel lanes are reversed is different from the experience. I think I was cringing for about the first ten or fifteen minutes. I did do some driving over there and still can shift a manual transmission vehicle with my left hand even after all these years.

In the meantime, that crew member was briefing me on the ship, the area, and all sorts of other things. I tried to absorb the information like a sponge and he answered the questions I had.

Having to go through British Customs whenever I had to go from the ship to shore or vice versa was a tad surprising, but very understandable.

I found the people to be very friendly folks. I did have a bit of adjusting to do to 'tune' my ear to the accent. I'm sure they had trouble with mine, and I was glad I did not have a US Southern accent! In time, my accent shifted to meet theirs.

I probably should indicate I was on the USS *Los Alamos* AFDB7 – the dry dock. Its crew numbered 165, versus the Tender's 1,500.

I did not want to leave when my time was up, but could not stay as my replacement already had his orders.

Scotland, and its people, are very, very fine and I take my hat off to both. It was quite a privilege and honour to be there. I was 18 years old when I arrived.

Liberty boats like the one below were a feature of daily life on the Holy Loch during the years of the Base. They were used to transport personnel from ship to shore. Jim Collins (left) whose job it was to sail these vessels

Lt Commander Rober t Jackson arrives early in Dunoon's Queen's Hall for the US Navy ceremony in 1992 to bid farewell to the Holy Loch after 31 years

The American Years

Afterword

Hundreds of marriages took place over the years and the personal bonds brought a network across the US and Scotland which continues today. Many a Dunoon family has American connections now and many are the parents who have travelled back and forth to the States over the years to see daughters and sons and grandchildren. They are as at home there now, as they are in Dunoon, in a way they may never have imagined.

In the early days, it was a daunting prospect to see a daughter marry a serviceman and leave for that far away future. Some Americans married local girls and stayed in Scotland. Some children of servicemen married Dunoonites, teenage love that blossomed into a life together. So the network grew, and when my husband and I travel in the States we are often amazed to meet people, in the most chance encounters, who know Dunoon, because of the years of the base. My own life, having married the son of a serviceman, has been endlessly enriched by travel to the US and the warm and loving relatives and friends I have gained. We both learn from one another. All of us who have gained these connections have had our horizons broadened and have experienced the fuller picture of this huge country outside of the military.

When the Base left the Holy Loch in June 1992 with much ceremony, there were strange mixed feelings. It had been there much longer than anyone had ever expected. The world had changed and was a much smaller place. Our lives had more in common and we knew each others' ways. Latterly US personnel had a much lower profile in the town. There were still resentments and not every American had liked it in Scotland. Some Dunoon people felt it had contributed nothing to the local economy, indeed it had ruined the town and used up education and health resources. Others felt it had brought some sort of prosperity through lean years and given local people employment and a chance to earn and spend locally.

But the Holy Loch looked strangely empty where it had once teemed with life and there was silence without the Liberty boats. When the rental properties filled with incomers and crime seemed to rise through the nineties, people said they wished the Americans were still there. The town seemed eerily quiet. A whole community had suddenly disappeared from our midst. Post mortems on the past began, and business people fretted over the future. It was an insecure time in the wake of such a high level of dependency on the presence of several thousand Americans. In the years since their departure, many family businesses have given up.

The interesting thing is that ex-Holy Loch servicemen keep in touch and hold regular reunions in Dunoon and that their children seem to want to revisit the scenes of their youth.

USS *Proteus* in Holy Loch

US Navy FBM Submarine Tenders and Submarines in the Holy Loch 1961–1992

The Fleet Ballistic Missile (FBM) submarine programme was undertaken in 1956 to utilise the nuclear submarine's capability of prolonged submerged patrols. The first US Ship Submersible Ballistic (Nuclear) (SSBN) submarine USS *George Washington* (SSBN 598) was constructed from the keel of a Hunter Killer type at the very end of 1957. The hull was lengthened by 130 ft to install the 'Sherwood Forest' where 16 launch tubes held A-1 missiles, each with a single W-47 (600 kT) thermonuclear warhead. The Washington Class had a complement of 13 Officers, 124 enlisted, 2 crews Blue and Gold.

The Polaris A1 was the first missile in the world to have the capability of underwater launch in the strategic deterrence developed by the US and USSR in the Cold War. A previous submarine launched missile, the Regulus, had required to be launched while the Sub was surfaced. This was used by the Soviet Navy until 1963. The method used by the US to circumvent the problem of igniting missile fuel inside a submarine was the so-called 'cold launch'. Gas pressure propelled the missile out of the vertical launch tube. A solid-fuel, Submarine Launched Ballistic Missile (SLBM), the A1 weighed 28,800 lb, with a length 28.5 ft and diameter 54 in, it had a range of approximately 1380 statute miles. The first stage (18,400 lb) had a steel motor case; polyurethane propellant (15,200 lb) with ammonium percholorate (oxidizer) and aluminum additives. The second stage (9,400 lb) also used a steel motor case; polyurethane propellant (7,300 lb) with ammonium perchlorate (oxidizer) and aluminum additives. It had an accuracy of 900m Circular Error Probable (CEP) at full range.

The next step was to enhance the Polaris A-3 by cutting down on its weight, an improved second stage motor with more efficient propellant and thrust vectoring control. This increased the range to 4600km. The warhead section now had three re-entry vehicles each carrying a 200kT W-58 warhead. The inertial guidance system lowered the Circular Error Probable (CEP) to 600m. The Polaris A-3 was operational from mid 1964 aboard USS *Daniel Webster* (SSBN-626).

Poseidon C-3

The Polaris A-3 was succeeded by the Poseidon C-3 missile. It was a development of a missile to the greatest dimensions allowable in the Polaris missile tubes with an accuracy of about 550m CEP with bigger warhead section. Poseidon C-3 had a payload of 10 to 14 independently targeted re-entry vehicles with W-68 thermonuclear (50 kT) warheads. Its maximum range was 5280km, reduced to 4000km with 14 re-entry vehicles. The purpose of low yield SLBMs being to destroy soft targets like cities, the precision of the weapons was not important. In fact, the strategy was not to be able to use it against hardened strategic targets as it was feared the Soviets would see the SSBNs as first strike capable and heighten tension. Destabilisation of the Mutual Assured Destruction (MAD) strategy adopted by both the USA and USSR was not attempted.

Poseidon had early problems with quality assurance and reliability of components, even including the nuclear warheads.

Trident I C-4 and Trident II D-5

The next strategic step in missile development was to increase the range substantially. It was decided to do this in two stages. The first stage was to develop the concept of Poseidon to include the use of existing SSBNs with their limited space in their missile compartments. Then it would be more cost-effective to decommission older boats and replace them with a new class of FBM submarines, the Ohio class. With the substantial lengthening of the range of SLBM missiles, the network of advanced bases like the Holy Loch was coming to an end. Trident was never supported at the Holy Loch.

In October 1979, SSBN- 657 became the first submarine to go on patrol with the Trident I C-4.

USS *Proteus* (AS-19)
Motto 'Prepared Productive Precise'

Commissioned 31 January 1944, in Oakland CA, her first operational port was Midway Island. She supported many submarines and gradually moved closer to Japan ending up in Tokyo Harbour for the surrender of the Japanese. Eventually, she became the support submarine tender at New London CT until January 1959 when she was ordered to Charleston SC to be put in dry dock and converted to support Polaris fleet ballistic missile submarines. The conversion added a 44 ft. section where a magazine designed to hold twenty spare missiles was built into the ship. As well as a huge crane, specialist workshops and additional generating capacity the *Proteus* was given the capacity to support nuclear power plant maintenance. She completed her first SSBN refit February 1961 and then moved onto Holy Loch, Scotland to support Submarine Squadron 14 (SubRon 14). Her arrival on 3rd March 1961 recommenced Dunoon and district's history with a submarine refit ship in the Holy Loch. During World War II the Holy Loch had also been a submarine support area. HMS *Forth* and *Titania* supporting the 3rd and 2nd Submarine Flotillas from Dec 1941 until 1945.

Proteus, with the Squadron Commodore based onboard, quickly built up the strength of SubRon 14 to 10 boats by December 1963. The strength of the squadron varied over its lifetime with brief visits from attack submarines, submarine rescue vessels, research submarines, Military Sealift Command transport ships (TAK) and many visiting naval and civilian dignitaries.

The American Years

Proteus went on to establish two further SSBN sites at Rota, Spain and Apra Harbor, Guam.

Proteus had supported submarines at Apra during World War II. Towards the end of 1961 the floating drydock, USS *Los Alamos* (AFDB-7) was towed into the Loch and assembled out of five sections by US Navy Seabees. The US Naval Support Activity was established ashore at Ardnadam hotel. It consisted of an exchange and commissary. Later the base housed about 2,000 American personnel with 1,600 dependents and employed about 150 Scottish workers. USS *Hunley* arrived 9th January 1963 and officially relieved *Proteus* 15th March 1963.

USS *Hunley* (AS 31)
Motto 'We Serve to Preserve Peace'
& USS *Holland* (AS 32) Motto 'World's Greatest Tender'

The Hunley class were the first US submarine tenders of post-World War II construction. The *Hunley* was commissioned June 1962, with a complement of approximately 1200 (54 officers). There were 52 separate workshops to provide mechanical and electrical support. The workshops could fabricate or repair most items. Repairs underwater, alongside the tender were possible by divers. Divers proved it possible to even replace a submarine propeller while alongside the tender. The original class crane was a 32 ton capacity hammerhead mounted aft of the missile compartment. This was changed to two 30 ton capacity cranes in 1967. The conversion to handle Poseidon C-3 missiles was carried out in 1974/75

In July 1966, USS *Simon Lake* relieved *Hunley*.

In 1982 *Hunley* was back at the Holy Loch until 1987.

Holland was at Holy Loch November 1975 until 1982.

USS *Simon Lake* (AS-33)
Motto 'Results Not Excuses'
& **USS *Canopus*** (AS-34)
Motto 'To Serve Ready for Service'

Simon Lake was commissioned November 1964. Her fellow class submarine tender *Canopus* was commissioned a year later. Designed to support three submarines alongside with a complement of 1400 (56 officers), they were equipped with two 30 ton cranes and 4 five ton mobile cranes. They were converted for Poseidon C-3 missile handling and repair in 1970/71. A further conversion to support Trident C-4 missiles was undertaken by *Simon Lake* in 1978, *Canopus* in 1984.

Simon Lake was at Holy Loch from July 1966 until 1970 and again 1987 to 1992, being the last tender at Holy Loch.

FBM Classes

George Washington (SSBN 598)
5 in class; Commissioned 12/59; Displacement 6,700 tons; Length 380 ft; Complement 100 Enlisted, 12 Officers

Ethan Allen (SSBN 608)
5 in class; Commissioned 9/61; Displacement 7,900 tons; Length 410 ft.

Lafayette (SSBN 616)
19 in class; Commissioned 4/63; Displacement 8250 tons; Length 425 ft; Complement 138

Benjamin Franklin (SSBN 640)
12 in class; Commissioned 10/65; Displacement 8250 tons; Length 425 ft; Complement 14 Officers 124 enlisted in 2 crews; Polaris A3 missiles; 5/72 Poseidon conversion; 11/79 Trident 1 conversion

Ohio (SSBN 726)
18 in class; Commissioned 11/81; Displacement 18,750 tons; Length 560 ft.

Current Status of US Nuclear deterrence

The US Navy's 18 Ohio-class nuclear-powered ballistic missile submarines (SSBN) carry a total of 408 Trident-1 and Trident-II submarine-launched ballistic missiles (SLBM), each with between five and eight warheads. The US State Department declared in December 2001 that the SSBN force carried a total of 3,120 warheads. The Navy is currently upgrading the Trident-II SLBMs to extend service life. Four SSBNs will be removed from service by 2007.

Index